MOVE THE NEEDLE

Lisa Jackson Tresch

MOVE THE NEEDLE

A Nonprofit Founder's Story of Seamstress
Apprenticeships, Peddling Products, and the Need to
Make a Difference

Lisa Jackson Tresch

STORIA PUBLISHING

Tulsa, OK

Move the Needle is a work of nonfiction. The events and conversations in this book have been set down to the best of the author's ability, although some names and details have been changed to protect the privacy of individuals.

Library of Congress Control Number: 2022902998

ISBN: 979-8-9857364-0-3

Book design by Megan Morrow

Published in the United States by Storia Publishing

www.storiawriter.com

www.lisajacksontresch.com

TABLE OF CONTENTS

for Kyle

In our beginnings lies our journey's end.

–Kofi Awoonor

INTRODUCTION

"I don't sew." This is how I start presentations about our nonprofit, so it seems fitting to begin this book with the same disclaimer. This is not a tale of my sewing adventures, but a memoir about founding and directing a small nonprofit. I stumbled my way into it, and learned that for many women around the world, learning to sew can move them closer to a life of self-sufficiency. And I discovered that directing a nonprofit is a lot like keeping the machine running—a stitch at a time, and maybe ripping the entire project apart a few times.

But the sewing part of this story comes later. The beginning is in 1972 on Sunset Lane in Elk City, Oklahoma, a place with flat land, red dirt, and kind-hearted people. This is the setting where my memories begin and take shape. On summer days, my friends and I scoured our neighborhood for adventures, barefoot and sheltered in our small red-dirt community. One of my first memories is traveling with my mother across town to deliver clothes to a family with a houseful of children. It's a hazy memory with little detail, but it must have planted a seed in me. A few years later, when I was seven years old, I left my house on a Sunday afternoon with an empty coffee can in my hand. My friend Lori lived a few doors down, and I dragged her out on a mission to fill the can with coins and bills. We knocked on the doors of our kind-hearted neighbors and told them we were raising money for poor children. It's possible the idea came from my trip across town with my mother to deliver those clothes, but I can't be sure. We lived an insulated, middle-class life, but most children have an innate sense of justice and are not shy to demand that someone fix what seems unfair. Or maybe I was restless and unable to sit still. Sometimes it's hard for me to know the difference.

I returned with my coffee can overflowing and announced my plan to give the money to poor children in our town, whoever they might be. Without discussion, Dad took the can and sent its contents to the muscular dystrophy society, which was receiving the money raised from the golf tournament he watched that Saturday afternoon.

"Do not ask people for money," Dad said, but now I can't recall whether he was angry. After all, how can you begrudge good intentions? He probably spent the next few weeks apologizing to the neighbors and then had to take back his words thirty years later when I started asking people for money again. I have spent most of my adult life with the figurative coffee can in hand, convinced I could save a corner of the world if enough people joined my cause. After being raised in church, I stayed there for most of my adult life. It was a place with ample opportunities to replicate my jaunt around the neighborhood with Lori, but this time, the border went far beyond the streets adjacent to Sunset Lane.

I inserted myself into causes that required fundraising, like the time we traveled to a mental hospital in Azerbaijan and found that the women's wing had original, drafty windows while the men's wing enjoyed new, double-paned glass that kept them warm through the harsh winters. This injustice had to be fixed, so I made notecards with photos of the female patients' art and distributed them to our travel team in bundles of eight. We kept printing and selling until we had raised enough money to purchase and install those windows.

In my mid-forties, I had slowed my traveling and landed in a comfortable place as a wife, mother, and magazine editor. Writing quelled my restlessness, so I gave myself over to it and settled in for a season. But I was never without a nervous twitch, always ready to jump into a cause and help fix something that seemed broken.

In May 2012, I was volunteering with a local international adoption agency and met an older couple from Ghana, Peter and Anna. They were in Tulsa for an afternoon, visiting the agency to discuss school-age orphaned children who needed to find a permanent living situation. In the meantime, the children also needed sponsors to cover their school fees so they weren't forced to drop out. Peter placed photos of six wide-eyed children on the long conference table where we met and told us they were living in an orphanage, but the parents were still alive. For about half an hour, he did his best to answer my questions about the children and their parents, then said, "Come to Ghana. It will explain many things." During the meeting, Peter invited me to visit his country at least ten times and by the end, I was asking him about weather, flight options and the best time of the year to travel.

My life didn't feel dull, just comfortable, but maybe that was the problem. Comfort has always produced in me restlessness with a touch of guilt, which usually gets me moving. Traveling to Ghana and meeting the children could be an opportunity to write, raise awareness about Peter's nonprofit, and find education sponsors for the children, none of whom were in school. I accepted his invitation and dragged my oldest daughter, Erin, with me to Ankaase, a village in the Ashanti region where Peter was raised. I took my computer and a fancy camera so I could document my trip and write a magazine article that might secure sponsors for the children. Then, I would return to Tulsa and settle back in.

I felt at home surrounded by the red dirt of Ghana. It's filled with iron and aluminum, which, mixed with heavy rainfalls and intense heat, produces a deep, orange-red hue that stains the bottom of bare feet after a day of walking. Many of the houses are constructed with this red clay, formed into mud bricks, and roofed with thatch. Dotted between the red brick houses are cinder block or cement structures painted vibrant colors of red, green, yellow, and blue.

"I remember this dirt," I told Erin. "I grew up with it."

Together, we stood in that crowded town on a red dirt road, our skin glaringly white and our souls exceedingly hopeful.

A decade earlier, Peter and Anna had formed a Non-Governmental Organization in Ghana to help students in villages near the city of Kumasi. They were both former teachers, and Peter was proud of the tagline for his organization: "Education is the key to life." It was a declarative statement that some might find argument with, but in Ghana, there were more risks and dead-ends if a child was dropping in and out of school every year. Peter was hopeful I could bring awareness to the plight of children who needed sponsors, and find more financial resources in the U.S. for his organization. He knew that the best way for me to see the needs of the families up close was to take me to their homes.

Two days after we arrived, we sat in a semi-circle in front of a cinder block house, waiting to visit with one of those families. It had taken 20 minutes to find enough plastic chairs, gather the relatives, and decide where each of us should sit. In early May, like most other months, the air in Ghana is thick with humidity and sweat ran down my back into the waistband of my skirt. I leaned forward in my chair to keep my back from touching the hot plastic. We had been waiting to start our visit with the large family seated around us, but no one made a move to begin, so I stepped over to Peter's chair, crouching as I walked, out of place and obvious.

"Are they waiting for us or are we waiting for them?" I whispered.

"We're waiting for the grandmother," he whispered back. "We can't start without her."

I crouched my way back to the baking plastic chair, an impatient Westerner who didn't know the first thing about Ghanaian protocol and etiquette. I smiled apologetically at the oldest son, who nodded back at me. The family matriarch finally shuffled from a field behind the small, one-room structure where six of the family members lived. She sat down hard and graced me with a toothless smile.

I expected Peter to begin the conversation, but instead, each family member stood up, and in a single file line, shook our hand and greeted us with "Akwaaba," the Twi word for welcome.

My mind went blank. "Akwaaba," I replied, unable to remember the word for "thank you." I had studied my vocabulary index cards on the plane, but the simple word, "Medaase," eluded me that day. I blamed it on the humidity, jet lag, culture shock.

After family members sat back down, the elder grandmother spoke in Twi to Peter, who then turned to me and said in his booming voice, "They are asking, 'what is the news from the road?'"

Peter had prepped me for the question, but it still surprised me. What road? Which news? Maybe they wanted to know my reason for being here, which wasn't straightforward. Peter had invited me to come meet the children, and without a second thought, I booked a flight and dragged Erin along. But at that moment, with ten sets of eyes staring at me, I blanked. *I'm here to write a magazine article*, didn't feel quite right. *I'm restless and believe I can help save the world*, might have been closer to the truth, but not the answer I would ever voice. Did I really know why I had rushed to accept Peter's invitation? The family waited patiently, including the grandmother who had left her work in the fields to come meet me. I needed to come up with some news from the road.

"I bring greetings from friends in the United States," I said, sounding like I had landed on another planet, an alien explaining why she was invading a place that never asked for her presence. My daughter raised her eyebrows and swatted at a fly.

"I'm here to learn," I continued, which was the truth. "And I want to help the children, but I'm not sure where to start."

Peter translated, and the family members contemplated the

ground as he spoke. He went on for a while, and I wondered if he was clarifying my disappointing answer.

You will know the way forward," Peter said, while the adults in the family smiled and nodded. This is a common refrain in Ghana, a phrase that implies it is okay to wait for answers to be revealed, ideas to simmer, someone to help us discover which road to take. I prefer the quick fix so I can get on with things. But that day, as I sat on the red dirt in front of a house made from mud bricks, I felt the weight of making promises I couldn't keep. And I didn't have answers or ideas. Not yet. It was a weight I would feel many times as I traveled back and forth to Ankaase and other villages in Ghana.

Eighteen months after my first visit, I found a way forward by linking arms with another Ghanaian and starting a nonprofit, which planted my feet even further into that red dirt.

On numerous trips to Ghana, people would ask me to share news from the road every time we sat in a circle in front of a villager's house. And every time, I stumbled around my answer. It took me a decade to understand that the question wasn't a request for me to share travel adventures or my vision for making a big difference. It was a simple desire to hear my story. They weren't asking for promises; they wanted to know what I had learned on my journey. What happened on the road that was worth sharing?

This book is my attempt to answer that question. What happened over the next eight years is not what I would have imagined it to be when I decided to start a nonprofit. Sometimes I made things better, other times I created a mess. Some days I felt like giving up, and other days my heart broke in ways that made me furious enough to continue.

This is a story about how I found a corner of the world where sewing machines were an entryway to a better life for a mother and a child, and then how I came back home to discover it all over again. In the process, I learned how to be content with small, incremental changes—in our nonprofit's work and in my own life. Grab a plastic chair and let's make a circle in the red dirt of your imagination. I have news from the road.

CHAPTER ONE

A Tenuous Place

BLOG POST, MAY 16, 2012

Hooray for Wi-fi! Such small extravagances seem huge tonight.

Photos, however, are just not happening. The Wi-fi is very sleepy and keeps drifting in and out.

Today, we rode a bus to Kumasi. That's it. You can only plan about one activity a day here. It's a combination of traffic snarls (what Peter calls, "go slow traffic"), and just general delays that are mostly un- explained. Everything moves at a pace that suggests that this might be a good day for that activity—but tomorrow would be just as good. It doesn't really matter.

But today was a good day to take a bus to Kumasi, so that's what we did for six and a half hours. I won't explain the traffic delays; they're so common as to be mundane. But here is a little Ghana thing I love: slogans on the back of tro-tros (overcrowded minibuses) and taxis. The slogans are lettered on the back window. A sampling:

He's Able

By the Power of God

Do Unto Others

God is in Control

As If But Not (?)

Jesus is Coming

Pray for Drivers

And my personal favorite: **Just a Day**. *I'd like to meet the guy who decided on that one amidst all the super-spiritual ones beside him on the road. "Think I'll just tell it like it is," he might have said. "After all, it's just a day."*

So today, in Ghana, it was just a day. We sat on the bus, amazed that there was not one stretch between Accra and Kumasi where we didn't see people walking along the shoulder of the highway: groups of schoolchildren, mothers with babies strapped on their backs, men lying on mats, women strolling together with water containers on their heads. People, especially children, are everywhere. In the small villages along the highway, they all seem to be in close community— groups of ten or more sitting together talking, laughing and watching the children scamper around—like mini campgrounds along the way. This is a culture that values community and it was evidenced on our long route, from one city to the next. For each one of these people, it was "just a day."

It's easy for me to get lost in my surroundings because I'm people-watching. On my first trip to Ghana, Erin, Peter, and I arrived in Kumasi late in the day, after a six-hour bus trip from the coastal capital city of Accra to the interior of the Ashanti region. Peter and Anna had arranged for us to tutor children at the Seventh Day Adventist School in Ankaase, meet their families, and learn about rural Ghanaian culture. My education began before I stepped off the bus as I watched a crowd of women rush to the cargo area below us. Even now, I don't know where the bus from Accra to Kumasi drops off passengers because I couldn't take my eyes off those women.

They were yelling and pushing one another out of the way, babies tied on their backs with a colorful swath of fabric. The women wanted to unload our suitcases, hoping we would throw them a *pesawa*, or if God showed them favor, an American dollar. They were thin, and some were barefoot, their feet caked with red dirt. I was mesmerized.

"Who are they?" I asked Peter, looking through the window at the women below us. The bus driver had hurried out to swat at them, as if the women were pesky flies in his kitchen. They cowered away from the driver, still yelling at one another as they scattered.

"Petty traders," Peter answered. "It's a terrible job for a woman, but for most of them, there aren't other good options."

I would soon learn more about petty trading and how society views women who are forced into this type of work, but that day I witnessed what a mother in Ghana would do to feed her child. Petty traders worked in every city, town and village, balancing on their heads large bowls filled with garden produce and goods imported from foreign countries. In the rural areas, the traders were all women. This type of business is small-scale and in-formal, requiring minimal investment but providing unreliable income. Many women struggle to eke out a living, hoping to turn their micro-business into a bigger venture, which rarely happens. The women have low levels of education and almost no access to larger lines of credit, so kick-starting a business is virtually impossible. They can buy a small amount of inventory on credit, but then it's hard to scale the business. Once they pay off creditors, they are selling to generate daily subsistence, and the income earned will always be minimal.

As we descended the stairs of the bus and out into the commotion of Kumasi, I looked for the women who competed to carry our luggage, but they had disappeared into the crowds. I would never forget the desperation in their movements as they pushed and shoved, jostling for the right to earn any amount of income. The babies were nestled within the folds of the batik fabric and against the strong backs of their mothers, but it was a tenuous place for both of them.

The day I booked a flight to Ghana, I knew nothing about the struggles women face in rural villages; nothing about the mothers in these communities who worry they won't be able to pay school fees or feed their children. We went because of six children whose photos I had scattered across my kitchen table, many of them smiling awkwardly like my own children when the camera appeared. They lived in orphanages for months during the year, times when their mothers or relatives couldn't afford the basics—school fees, enough food, decent clothing. The children were in and out, not orphans, but not permanent family members either. Samuel, wearing a red shirt and holding a Bible upside down, was ten and had been shuffled from an orphanage, back to his mother, and finally to his grandmother. She had few resources and struggled to feed herself and the other relatives who lived with her.

On our first day of tutoring, Erin and I arrived at the school with our supplies, my camera, and a shared feeling that we were out of our element. Neither of us were teachers, so we walked into that Ghanaian classroom and turned in circles a few times before we saw Samuel, the one with the upside-down Bible. He was sitting beside a lanky young man, reading to him in Twi.

"Hello," Erin and I said in unison, unintentionally, but it made the boys smile. They stood up, and I noticed that Samuel's school uniform shirt was backwards and inside out. His socks had been white in the past, but were now gray, and his shoes were too big. Osei was the young man sitting next to Samuel. His photo had not been on my kitchen table, but after we arrived in Ghana, Peter asked if we would tutor him as well. He was eighteen years old and obsessed with soccer. Osei's family had pulled him out of school in the third grade to work on his grand-parent's small farm, because sometimes a family must choose between a child's education or his value as a laborer. Osei didn't read, write, or speak English, and for reasons I couldn't fathom, had agreed to be placed in a third-grade classroom where he towered over the other students. Two girls, Sarah and Beatrice, joined us, and then another young boy, Kadri. For five days, we created words from spongy letters and formed sentences using square tiles. By the end of the week, we progressed to creative, nonsense sentences that made us all laugh, which we decided was more important than trying to explain grammatical structure.

The cat is blue. The sun is a bike. Pigs can dance.

When we visited Samuel's home after tutoring one afternoon and met his grandmother, Peter told me not to ask about his mother, so I didn't. Later that evening, over a meal of *banku* and tilapia, Peter talked about mothers trapped in risky occupations because they have no other way to care for their children. "What can we do for them?" I asked, and he replied, "They need good jobs. Not petty trading or work that puts them in danger."

A few days later, we visited Peter and Anna's relatives in a small, lively farming village outside Ankaase. Groups of women had gathered their wares on benches between houses, trying to sell everything from plastic shoes to plantains. Cocoa beans were drying on a large slab of plywood in the center of the village, and colorful clothes hung on drying lines in front of cinder block and mud brick homes. Cooking fires burned in front of most of the homes, and a few pairs of women were pounding *fufu*. In between two houses, I noticed a little boy of about two wearing an oversized shirt and constructing a push car out of a large yellow plastic jug and a flattened cardboard box. He was intent on forming a seat from the cardboard and after he was successful, he began pushing his makeshift car around in the dirt. I snapped several photos until his mother walked over to our group. She glanced at me several times as she talked with Anna. At first, I thought she approached us because I upset her by taking photos of her child, but I had asked permission, and she was smiling.

"Is everything okay?" I asked Anna.

"Yes. She just wanted to ask if you will take him with you."

I put down my camera and looked at the boy's mother, who was bobbing her head up and down. Anna spoke to her in Twi and the woman's smile disappeared. She held out her arm and jabbed her finger toward the little boy, who was oblivious and still pushing his car. Anna spoke to her again, shaking her head and gesturing at me. The woman's smile returned, and she waved goodbye.

It had all been surreal.

"If we had said yes, would she let him walk away with us?" I asked.

Anna told me it was possible. "We must understand why she is making the request. She loves him, but she believes he would have a better life in the U.S."

It happened three other times during our trip. I never got used to the mothers who would ask if I would take their children. After I wrote a series of blog posts about this, people who were reading had opinions. They wanted to talk about what makes a good parent.

"How could a mother give up her child?" A woman asked after I spoke at a fundraising event between trips. "That's just not natural."

While I had been standing in front of that mother's house in Ghana, trying to process her request that I take her son, I didn't notice her dress hanging from bony shoulders and the dark circles under her eyes. It was only when I studied the photo a few evenings later that I saw how tired she looked. I sympathize with people who don't understand how a mother could give up her child, but I also know it's a privilege to even ask the question.

We form our conception of good parenting from the reality of our circumstances. If we never face the frightening possibility that our child might go hungry tomorrow, we can't comprehend how handing the child to a relative, an orphanage, or someone on another continent seems like a solution. My "can-do" spirit tells me there must be another way. But I learned that for many women in Ghana, good options are scarce. Men had the freedom to walk away from their families, and for those who stayed, surviving off the land became harder every year. Either way, the women were responsible for feeding and educating the children, and that's a challenge when you're selling hair accessories or plastic shoes to people who have seen you five times already that day. Most banks didn't give women credit to start businesses, which put the dream far out of reach for them.

I wanted to find a happy ending for Adu, Osei, Sarah, Beatrice, Kadri and the other children whose mothers could no longer care for them. Some of the younger children were available for adoption, but the trauma of being removed from your village and plopped into a new culture might last for years, or a lifetime. Six months after my first trip to Ghana, I escorted one of the orphaned children, a six-year-old girl, from her village into waiting arms of adoptive parents in the U.S. Throughout the flight, she cried, refused the food, and asked in Twi if she could go back home. She would soon be part of a loving family that would give her everything she needed, but on that flight, as she laid with her head in my lap and her tears streaming across my legs, it didn't feel like a happy ending. I wanted to turn around, take her home, and find a way for the mothers to keep their children.

Peter and I talked about the progress Ghana had made in economic growth, but it wasn't trickling down to the rural areas or into the lives of the women in villages like Ankaase. With little access to capital, they struggled to start businesses, which was the only path to sustainable income for most women. In the afternoons, we would walk along the dirt roads in the village while Peter talked to me about the struggles of families who didn't have access to education. The women were at risk of becoming desperate enough to work dangerous jobs, the children vulnerable to traffickers. One afternoon, I noticed a group of women sewing on the covered front area of a house and commented on the familiar black machines in front of them. "My mother sewed on one just like those," I told him.

The women were turning the round crank with one hand and pushing fabric through the sewing needle with the other. I've tried this and failed. It takes a level of coordination I do not possess, sort of like the head rubbing and stomach patting we tried as children. Some people can do this with ease, but I was the one with both hands, either patting or rubbing because I couldn't do both. These women were able to crank the handle, guide fabric, and carry on energetic conversations at the same time. There were yards of colorful cloth stacked on tables beside them, and two children sitting on the ground sharing a bag of dried plantains.

"That's Hildy and her apprentices," Peter said.

"Can I meet her?"

Hildy and the women were polite, but also busy, so I couldn't ask all the questions running through my head: *How does a woman become an apprentice? How would she start a sewing business in a rural village? And how did you learn to move your hands in two different directions?*

"Come back," Peter said, which he had been repeating for the seven days we were in Ghana. "You have much more to learn."

Erin and I flew home on a Thursday. We left about half of what we brought over with Peter and asked him to distribute it to the children. Gifts, t-shirts, school supplies, soccer balls, and books. Something had been wrenched out of me and left there as well, but I didn't want to reduce it to a trite, "I left part of my heart in Ghana." Some of us think we are here to do big things, so we identify imperfect situations and charge in with certainty. I went to Ghana for the first time because of the children, but I couldn't look away from the mothers. The image of Hildy and the apprentices was a bright contrast to the desperate women who had surrounded our bus the day we arrived in Kumasi. When I pictured those women seated at a sewing machine, laughing with colorful fabric under the needle, the injustice seemed fixable, the lofty goals worthy of at least giving them a shot. I think this is always how it starts, with such assurance that our big ideas can sprout wings and fly. I'm a fixer, but I probably could have found a simpler place to start.

BLOG POST, OCTOBER 4, 2012

It was a sweltering afternoon in Ankaase and the temperature in the schoolroom was even hotter, but at least we were inside. The sun in Ghana is like a different star than it is at home: closer, brighter, and with the kind of heat that reminds you how small and vulnerable you are. I grabbed a bottle of Coke (not Diet Coke, not Coke Zero, but sugar-laden Coke) and drank it like water. The sweet drink was a gift, brought to us as part of a goodbye ceremony. We were spending our last day with the children in the SDA school—giving and receiving parting gifts, taking photos, giving brief speeches, and drinking our Cokes. At the end of the ceremony, Daniel, the school headmaster and our new friend, handed us a carved bird with its head turned back toward its tail.

"It's Sankofa," Daniel said as he handed the wood carving to me with both hands. "It means we wish you will always remember us and

come back to us." I accepted the gift but didn't fully understand its significance. I packed my carved bird, brought it back to the U.S., and put it on a shelf that housed my knick-knacks. Then I kind of forgot about Sankofa.

Several months ago, I began considering a return to this small village. As I continued to learn more of the children's stories and hear of the needs, I realized that there was something else for me to do in Ankaase. Maybe more than one something. There are those seasons of life when things feel out of your control, and I am right in the middle of one of those.

Recently, I ran across a video that included an interview with a bead seller in Ghana. "For a while, we shunned the beads," she said in the interview. "People thought they were archaic, or unfashionable. But we have a culture of Sankofa—go back and retrieve what you left behind— and now people are returning to the beads."

Sankofa. Where had I heard that before? And then I remembered my carved bird. I jumped up and pulled it from the shelf. "Go back and retrieve what you left behind," or the literal translation: "It is not wrong to go back for what is at risk of being left behind."

I got the message.

So, I'm going back to Ghana on October 17. This time, Erin will stay here, and I will travel with our friends Peter and Anna. I'll be staying in a cool little African bungalow with a cat named Tooles (forgive me, kitty, if I have the spelling wrong). I'll be blogging here and praying that my cable modem will work in the village. I hope you'll join me as I return for what is at risk of being left behind.

CHAPTER TWO

Dopamine

BLOG POST, OCTOBER 24, 2012

Daniel, the headmaster, told us there was a big celebration planned for the computer presentation, but I wasn't sure exactly what that meant. He mentioned a band, a parade through the streets, dignitaries who would attend, and speeches that would be given. But, I was skeptical. Not to take away from the amazing outpouring of donors for the computers, but I couldn't imagine all that hoopla for six laptops. And three mice. Of course, I'm learning to suspend reality.

There was a parade. About 400 students were waiting on the main village road when we arrived by taxi, and we got out and walked with them to the site of the celebration. People lined the streets, including the village elders.

We arrived at the soccer field (futball pitch) where three tents were set up for the event: a main tent for dignitaries, the schoolchildren on one side, and parents and villagers on the other side. Someone introduced the dignitaries, which included elders, the deputy chief of the village, representatives from the Seventh Day Adventist Church and other religious places of worship, and school representatives for the region. There were also pastors and other important people who stood up to be recognized. I lost track. There were four long rows of VIPs. And there, front and center, was the ratty action packer I had brought the computers in, covered by a beautiful white and purple cloth. At that point, I wished I had borrowed a nicer action packer, but I also knew that no one in attendance would care one bit. So, I decided not to care either. I was beyond amazed, and what kept running through my mind throughout the ceremony was, "How on earth did I end up here?" And, I don't have a suitable answer for that.

If you and I were sitting in a circle on our plastic chairs, this part of "news from the road" is the story of getting sidetracked by a computer lab. After my first trip to Ghana, the headmaster of the SDA school asked Peter if his organization could help them start the lab. The government mandated that public schools in Ghana provide courses on computers but provided no computers or equipment. Teachers would sketch a picture of a keyboard on the blackboard and explain the keys and their functions. It was all theoretical, as if there were an actual computer in the room. The window message on a taxi in Kumasi, "As if, but not," seemed applicable here, and I wondered if the driver had been a former information technology instructor.

After the first trip to Ghana, I agreed to become a full-time volunteer with Peter's nonprofit organization, and my first project was to raise funds for a new computer lab. And that is how I ended up making a speech to half of Ankaase and the village dignitaries before receiving a ceremonial *Kente* cloth dress. It included a monogrammed sash: Jackson Tresch Lisa.

The crowd roared when Daniel dramatically dragged the cloth off the action packer, and right then, I was in over my head. Maybe one of those village chiefs should have demanded to see my long-term plan for the computer lab, or did I just come here for the parade? That would have been a fair question. It was easy to push the worries down when Otis, the Information Technology teacher, gave me a thumbs up. He would take care of getting everything set up and take it from there.

It was joyous and heady until I realized later in the week that we would also need scanners, projectors, more mouse pads and mice, printers, and a workaround for the frequent, but planned, government power outages. We worked it all out—sort of—but this should have raised a hundred red flags that my good intentions were bumping up against my cross-cultural acumen.

From that day forward, The Laptop Parade informed every decision about what I would do, and not do, in Ghana. During my next four trips, people would stop me as I walked through the village and ask for a laptop. "Serves you right," I told myself.

After a few years, I realized this was the rhythm my village friends and I danced to. They had a look in their eye that told me they didn't expect a laptop, but there was a type of justice in the asking. If you bring six laptops and unveil them ceremoniously in front of half the village, you're probably going to answer for it.

Part of the human brain, the nucleus accumbens, lights up when we give resources to other people. It's a kind of reward circuit that makes us feel good when we are generous, so if you bring six laptops and three mice to Ghana, you get a nice dopamine hit that will convince you to do it again. Later (sometimes much later) the brain dissects the consequences of this generosity and forces you to ask, "Is it always wise to hand over resources without considering long-term implications—even if it makes me feel good about doing good?"

These lessons take time because good feelings derived from giving are addictive. It's a type of high, and our brain wants it again, and then one more time. Not all generosity is self-serving, and I trust mine wasn't, but sometimes in the rush of receiving a Laptop Parade, the short-term euphoria is blinding. Our need to make a difference is why the world continues to be a place of hope, despite the destruction humanity is prone to bring on itself. We keep finding ways to fix the mess by making our corner of the world a little better. But sometimes I forgot Ghana wasn't my corner of the world, and I stumbled over the cultural blocks that kept showing up on the path.

Once I returned home, I was ready to go back. I didn't want another Laptop Parade, but I did want to learn what could be done to make a difference in the lives of struggling, single mothers. Helping them, however, was more complicated than raising money for a child's education or funding a computer lab. When Peter and Anna visited my house in Tulsa and gave me a *Krobo* bead bracelet, I wore it every day to remind myself to stay in the background, listen and learn. The way forward can be a slow process.

The Krobo beads were unlike any I had ever seen, so I did some research and learned they were made using an outdoor oven and broken glass. The process goes like this: gather old glass, something like Milk of Magnesia bottles—and Ponds Cold

Cream jars work well too. Crush the glass into a fine powder and then mix it with ceramic dye and pour the mixture into small molds. Insert a stick from a Cassava plant into the center of the mold mixture, take a large spatula and slide the molds into the clay oven, then fire the mixture. Wait a while. Then, slide the molds back out, remove each bead from the mold, slip out the Cassava stick and let the beads cool.

After washing the beads, the painting begins. After each layer of paint, the artist fires the beads again and at the end of the process, there is a pile of intricate, colorful beads, no two exactly alike.

I'm not a jewelry gal, but I wore my bracelet every day and when someone asked about it, I pointed out the metaphor. Take a broken beer bottle and make a beautiful bracelet. Take a broken situation and fix it; transform it into something beautiful. The metaphor held up, but its simplicity was deceptive.

After a few weeks of wearing my bracelet, the Krobo beads sparked an idea for how we could raise money for the additional needs of the computer lab. The lab was incomplete, and I felt responsible for finishing what I had started. Despite my history with the coffee can, the hardest part of nonprofit work for me is the straight out "ask" for money. I wring my hands over it and keep hearing my father's voice. *Don't ask people for money.* Even though, decades later, he gladly wrote checks to donate to our work in Ghana, I still apologized for asking and was quick to justify the need. Not only to him, but to everyone.

"Let's sell Krobo bead bracelets to raise money for the computer lab," I said to Peter and Anna the night before their visit was over. "People will buy them if they know the proceeds will help the children."

The good feeling of giving combined with that same reward circuit for shopping is a successful combination when you're raising money. The idea of selling Krobo bead bracelets also felt a little savvy, more like we were making an exchange rather than holding out our hands. We solicited funds—this is part of the nonprofit model —but never without an option to purchase something handmade.

I learned how to string the beads on stretchy elastic to make a simple bracelet, but it was unlike any piece of jewelry most people in the U.S. had seen. The chunky beads had an organic, cultural look, and the bracelets sold. We were able to provide more computer equipment, including a generator that would keep the lab from being at the mercy of daily power outages. The school arranged another parade, a ceremony with multiple dance ensembles, and a ribbon cutting. This time, Peter and his NGO were in the foreground, but the people knew where the laptops came from.

"My brother needs a computer," a young mother told me as we passed by her house. She was bent over a pot of boiling water, dipping clothing in and out of it. The baby strapped to her back bobbed her head side to side, sleeping through the movements of laundry day. "My brother wants to be a teacher."

After just finishing a ceremony where we had provided more computers and a generator, it was hard to tell her I couldn't bring her brother a laptop. I could. But I couldn't. I refused to disrespect the people who requested a computer by telling them if I brought one for them, I would have to bring one for everyone. Which could prompt a valid question, "Why not do that?"

In Ghana, it was easy to make promises during the emotion of the moment, when everything seemed possible if you just had enough faith. The Laptop Parade didn't completely suppress my tendency to over-promise, but it redirected how I thought about generosity. I had jumped into a country I knew little about, with a history of white people, like me, barging in to do good. The dopamine hit sure feels nice, but the long-term results may not.

When the needs are so basic, it seems wrong not to hand someone a fix for the need. The education system in Ghana is full of contradictions. Education is the key to rising out of poverty, but the government doesn't fund the system in proportion to its necessity, especially in the rural villages. There seemed to be endless needs. Fix one problem (or just tell yourself you've fixed it) and five more rise to the surface. Large nonprofits and NGOs had the resources to wade into that quagmire, but Peter's organization didn't. And yet, the under-resourced rural schools were the glaring need that kept Peter's NGO begging for funds.

"Let's go to the orphanage and meet a mother and her baby," Peter said the morning after the second computer lab parade and celebration. "She wants to give her baby up for adoption. We should help her find a way forward."

This was a welcomed diversion from the computer lab. Not that I didn't care about technology, but the pull toward finding solutions for single mothers was growing stronger. I hoped that Peter's version of "find a way forward" meant something other than adoption. He had an interesting side job as a liaison for an international adoption agency, arranging placements for orphaned children in Ghana whose parents had died, or who had no caregivers to step in and raise them. Adoption was a solution that included heartbreak and joy, and I was never sure which of those emotions I felt more strongly. My youngest daughter

DOPAMINE | 41

and I are both adopted, so my feelings on this seem like they should be clear and unwavering, but they aren't.

The young mother was waiting for us in the dirt courtyard of the orphanage. Her hair was cropped close, like most of the girls in Ghana, and her baby wore tiny gold hoop earrings and a gauzy green dress. They were not what I expected. Peter talked to the orphanage director before he met with the woman, and I watched the young mother nuzzle her daughter's neck and breathe deeply, as if she were capturing the scent of this child she might relinquish.

Peter walked out into the courtyard of the orphanage and talked with her while I stood in the doorway. The mother shed tears, laughed, and was happily distracted by her baby while Peter talked with her. It was difficult to tell which direction it was going.

"What's the verdict?" I asked after she tied the baby on her back and left.

"This woman should find a way to keep her daughter. She has an older sister who could take the baby, but they had an argument and aren't talking to each other." Peter picked up his briefcase and slid his arms back into his suit coat. "I told her they should start talking."

"There's nothing else we can do?"

He shook his head.

"They need to work out their family disagreements. She has options, but many women don't, so let's focus on those women."

Anna and I had been working with the seamstress Hildy and her apprentices to make bags we would sell in the U.S. This was not a new idea. It seemed like everyone was bringing items back to the U.S. from far-flung places to sell at craft fairs or out of their garages. This type of altruistic retail benefits the women who make the products, the nonprofits who sell them, and people who want to shop and "do good" at the same time. Anna and I purchased fabric on the first day and delivered the stacks of batik and the pattern to Hildy's shop. The mother and daughter at the orphanage caused an idea to resurface, and I knew it wasn't going away, no matter how many computer lab needs and laptop parades were thrown in my path.

"Could we help a couple of women enter one of those apprenticeships?" I asked during dinner that evening. We were deep into bowls of groundnut soup and digging our fingers into doughy fufu. Peter and Anna had directed all their energies toward improving the village schools, and veering out of their lane wasn't so easy.

"I'll make sure the women get sponsors," I said. "You won't have to divide your energies between the apprenticeships and the schools, I promise."

Peter said nothing and took his time scooping the last bit of fufu from his bowl, then wiped his mouth and shrugged. "It might work."

"Maybe next trip?"

"Maybe."

I planned to schedule my trips to Ghana six months apart, which would give me time to think it through and make sure I wasn't rushing into anything. I wanted to talk more with Peter and Anna about the idea of resourcing apprenticeships before we launched a new program for his organization. The cook at the guesthouse, Esther, was serving bowls of fruit as we talked, and she seemed to like the idea.

Two days later, we attended the Methodist church in Ankaase, a beautiful rock building with a congregation comprising older women, a few young families, and lots of children. One of the pastors, Alberta, walked down the aisle before the service started and leaned over three older ladies who were sitting next to me in the pew. The pastor told me she had arranged a meeting of women who were interested in learning to sew and it would take place on the following Friday. Pastor Alberta spoke formally, as if we had already made this arrangement and she was confirming our plan. It was the Ankaase version of the phone game. Word had gotten out, but someone had the timeline wrong. We didn't have a program set up, and I was trying to learn my lesson about making promises I couldn't deliver on. I explained to her it wouldn't be possible on this trip.

"Oh, I'm so sorry," Pastor Alberta said. "The meeting has already been set."

The three older women were listening closely, and when one leaned over and whispered to another, I figured news about the meeting was about to spread further.

Over the next two days, I tried to cancel the meeting three times. The pastor told me the number of women had jumped from 10 to 15. She wasn't budging.

"The meeting," she repeated each time in her measured and polite voice, "has already been set." I gave in and decided that we would move forward because it was apparent once a meeting had been set, it cannot be changed. At least not this meeting.

On Thursday, Pastor Alberta told me she was traveling to another village and could not attend the Friday meeting.

"I'm sure you already know this, but I can't speak Twi." I tried not to sound panicky. "Can you please send a translator?"

She promised she would. My hands were sweating, and it felt like I was in over my head again. At least 15 women were going to show up and expect me to have resources in place to help them enter a sewing apprenticeship. We had connected with only one professional seamstress, and she had already filled her apprentice slots. We had nothing to offer the women.

Everything about this meeting and what might come of it felt completely out of my control. These are hard moments for me because I like control, or at least the illusion of it. Pastor Alberta's face softened, and she put her hand on my shoulder, looking at me steadily over her glasses. "I'll send someone to translate for you. His name is Isaac. He'll know what to do."

BLOG POST, OCTOBER 22, 2012

Today is one of those beautiful Saturdays when one of the college kids is home, we all slept in, fall is around the corner, and we're soaking in the good. This is when we feel comfortable and safe within our walls and with each other. Ah, I love it.

And then I remember that I'm leaving all of this on Wednesday and flying to Ghana. That doesn't feel comfortable or safe right now. It feels scary.

This is not the first time in preparing for this trip that I've had a moment of feeling like I'm insane. I felt it last time I traveled in May, so I should have known it was coming.

I should have remembered that any time I am leaning into things that hold me back, the fear factor settles in and whispers in my ear, "You're a little crazy." I have sudden anxieties about what might happen to my family while I'm gone, or what might happen to me, and I feel like I'm alone in the boat. In the midst of all the packing, preparing the computers, gathering items for the students, and all the other things that must be done before Wednesday, I find myself looking around my house today and thinking that the easiest thing for me to do would be to quit all this ridiculousness. Who am I kidding? I am inadequate to do the tasks that are laid out before me.

I'm trusting only a little today, hanging on by a thread. I want to curl up into a little ball on my couch with the cozy blanket and find a good Hallmark movie on cable. And I hate Hallmark movies. And cable.

CHAPTER THREE

Move Your Feet

BLOG POST, DECEMBER 17, 2012

I wrote in a previous post that I don't sew. My mother, however, was a dedicated seamstress for our family and she made quite a few of my clothes until I reached sixth grade and put my foot down: no more homemade attire. The wide-legged brown pants she made me that year garnered no compliments but only snide comments from peers concerning elephant legs. I was an adolescent with stocky thighs and calves (still have 'em) so these were mortifying moments. I put the pants in the hand-me-down bag as soon as I got home and nicely requested to my mother that she not make me any more clothes. As I made my request, I ignored the thought of her hunched over the old black Singer sewing machine that was on the dining room table dur-

ing sewing weeks. Of course, now the memory makes me want to hug every homemade article of clothing my mother stitched—if only I still had even one of them.

I also wrote in a previous post that I was traveling to Ghana in honor of my mother. That first trip I took last May had my mother's memory wrapped all around it for reasons I could not explain. Now, I think I have an explanation.

On January 7, Afia and Doris will begin their seamstress apprenticeship at Felicia's shop in the village of Ankaase, Ghana. My friends Diana and Janet will support them. And through the sale of our Ankaase bags, Isaac will be able to purchase each of them a chair, scissors, measuring tape, machine oil, pins, and a black Singer sewing machine just like the one my mother used. Mother never upgraded her machine, and now I'm thankful. Sometimes the very best gifts don't come wrapped up in packages and tied with a bow. Sometimes we don't even recognize them as gifts. They might come in the form of a meeting that "has already been set," a tiny sewing shop on the red-dirt streets of an African village, and two friends who opened their hearts to two women they might never meet.

Between October and March is the best time to visit Ghana because the temperatures are marginally cooler and less humid. Marginally. The Ankaase Methodist Church was stifling the afternoon of October 18, 2012, when we welcomed seventeen women into the sanctuary for interviews. They all arrived at the same time, streaming through the double doors of the sanctuary, carrying half-moon shaped straw fans and wary expressions. Many also carried a sleeping baby that was nestled in the batik fabric tied around their waist. Women in Ghana don't chit-chat. They are straight talkers, and if they have nothing to say, they are quiet. I was standing at the front of the sanctuary alone, waiting for Isaac, who, according to Pastor Alberta, would know what to do.

Since I didn't speak the women's language, I could only smile and nod. Some smiled back. Most looked at me suspiciously, and I couldn't blame them. They had gotten word that a Ghana NGO was going to choose two women to begin a seamstress apprentice program, and here was a white woman greeting them with a silent smile because she didn't speak their language.

The women had arrived about fifteen minutes before the appointed time, and when a young man walked through those same doors at exactly 10 a.m., the women were seated and waiting. He was young, wearing a crisp, pressed white shirt and jeans, and carrying a notebook and a pen. I felt like hugging him. He talked to the women as he walked up the aisle toward me, and I could see their body posture relax, and a few laughed and talked back to him. I didn't care what they were saying. There was a Ghanaian in the room who knew what to do, something I would never take for granted or believe I could do without.

I handed Isaac the questionnaire and asked him to please explain to the women there was nothing in place yet, that we would do the interviews, but it would take time to begin the program. He nodded understandingly and spoke in that fluid lilt of Twi, a tonal language which uses the pitch of the voice to distinguish between nouns, verbs and other grammatical information. It's a beautiful language, and as I stood listening, the cadence of the words calmed me.

The women didn't appear dissuaded by our disclaimer, so Isaac began the interviews, translating for me after each question and answer. He was soft-spoken and in no hurry. At first,

I was disappointed Pastor Alberta hadn't arranged for a woman to conduct the interviews, but as I watched how Isaac interacted with the women, I decided it didn't matter. He leaned in when they answered the questions, nodding with understanding while they shared their story. Each of the women had a reason to be in that church sanctuary, and Isaac's body language communicated that he cared. None of the women had anyone in their family willing or able to fund their entry into an apprenticeship. They had been trying to earn money in various ways—petty trading, selling fruits or vegetables at the market—but none of the work was steady. One woman and her mother lived in an abandoned house that had extensive fire damage. They were essentially homeless and her entry into an apprenticeship meant that in three years, someone in the family would earn a steady income. They would survive until then, but the apprenticeship was the escape route from homelessness. After Isaac finished interviewing the first three women, I relieved him of translating. We were all hot, and the babies were stirring.

"I trust you," I said to him. "You talk to them, and then you can guide me toward who we should choose."

Two hours later, the interviews ended, and Isaac mopped his face and neck with a large cloth he pulled from his bag. The women slowly walked back out the sanctuary's double doors as they talked and laughed, a few even smiling at me. Isaac had bridged a tiny part of the trust gap that day. The women had no reason to believe in me, but Isaac was one of them. They knew his father was the senior pastor of the Methodist church, that he worked at the hospital in Ankaase, and that he was willing to sit for two hours and patiently listen to the stories they told about their lives. Or maybe their smiles and laughter were from relief that the interviews were over.

He and I exited through the side door and walked down the dirt road that led back to the guest house.

"I want to help people in my village," he said. "I've been wishing to start some kind of organization to help families here."

There are many ways for an American to misstep in Ghana, and one of them is impulsivity. I'm prone to this because sometimes an idea seems too good not to work, but there are consequences to cultural blindness. When I blurted out that I would talk to Peter about him coming alongside and helping us, I forgot it doesn't always work like that. Peter and Isaac moved in different circles, and in Ghana, building trust with someone outside your circle takes time.

"I should have gone with you to those interviews," Peter told me later that night, after I explained my idea about bringing Isaac into his organization. "I don't know him well enough to bring him into what we're doing. You shouldn't have promised him anything."

He was right, but I was certain Isaac would help this new program take flight. We needed him. Peter was still skeptical about taking focus away from students, but I told him Isaac could direct his energies into running this new Income Generation program, and Peter and Anna could continue working with the children. I twisted Peter's arm, which I would later come to regret, but for now he had relented and allowed Isaac to join our work.

"You are too eager," Peter told me the next morning, pointing a finger at me like he was just figuring this out. "You have a lot to learn."

I couldn't have agreed more.

Sewing machines are everywhere in Ghana. In the rural villages, women put a wooden table on the dirt in front of their houses, set a sewing machine on the table and call it a business. And it is. The bright, colorful clothing with wild designs in the fabric makes our clothes in the U.S. look drab by comparison. Shopkeepers sell fabric in small markets, so if you want a custom dress, shirt, skirt, or pants, you purchase the fabric in one of the market stalls and take it to a professional seamstress or tailor.

Rural Ghanaians don't pop into Target for a piece of clothing. The closest option is the large urban market, where rows of discarded clothing from our closets are dumped for purchase. *New York Times* reporter George Packer says, "If you've ever left a bag of clothes outside the Salvation Army or given to a local church drive, chances are that you've dressed an African." Our donation centers are overloaded, so most of what we assume will stay local is pushed into a compressor that squeezes out neat cubes of secondhand clothing weighing a half ton each. Then the cubes are stacked and sent to textile recycling companies that designate four export classifications: "Premium" goes to Asia and Latin America; Africa A (clothes that have lost some brightness) goes to the better-off African countries like Kenya or Ghana; Africa B (clothes with a stain or small hole) goes to the continent's disaster areas such as DRC or Angola. Trade vendors wait at airports to sort through our stuff so they can haul it to local markets and make a buck. And what's so bad about that? Nothing until you peel back the layers. People in places like Ghana purchase our used clothing cheaper in the market than they would from a local textile manufacturer or a local seamstress, but the local textile manufacturing industry in Africa is on life-support.

Until the late 1990s, there were over 20 textile firms employing over 25,000 people, but by 2012, the country had only four textile factories employing less than 3,000 Ghanaians. Was there a cause and effect? I didn't know, but I had a guess. Local seamstresses made a decent living stitching the beautiful batik dresses, skirts, and shirts that were still popular traditional clothing, but they were always competing with the second-hand market vendors. If you could buy your little girl a pair of cheap studded jeans and a t-shirt that says "Flirt" for a fraction of the cost of a traditional wax fabric dress, maybe you would take that option.

I became interested in the textile industry just as we were starting our Income Generation program. As we planned our work with seamstress apprentices, I thought we could be a small part of helping Ghana revitalize a localized industry of making and purchasing clothing and accessories.

We welcomed Afia and Doris into the new Income Generation program as our first seamstress apprentices. In honor of our new program and these women, I decided to learn to sew during their first year of apprenticeship. A friend gave me an old 1970 cabinet machine that was so complicated I had to call my neighbor to thread it, so it didn't start well. I would teach myself, unlike the women in Ghana, who would learn from a professional seamstress named Felicia. The apprenticeship was a three-year program that would teach the women skills and show them what it takes to run a business. Like so many women in the rural areas of Ghana, Doris and Afia were eager to learn, but had little opportunity and no resources. The unpaid apprenticeship was an investment, which meant poor women without a family member who would sign as a guarantor couldn't enter. If a woman tried to learn on her own, she wouldn't receive the certificate of completion from the government, which would cause people to question her skills.

Isaac and I both wanted to see these women free themselves from dependency on charity and escape vulnerable situations. The investment for apprenticeship included a commitment fee paid to the professional seamstress, as well as the purchase of equipment, including a sewing machine. This expense was not a requirement for every apprenticeship program, but we wanted a woman to own a machine that she could take with her after training.

In many countries, especially in the Global South, sewing is a skill that is respected because it brings income. I grew up thinking of sewing as more of a hobby, even though my stay-at-home mother made my clothes for me. When I told her I no longer wanted apparel made on our dining room table, we marched into Penny's or Sears at the start of each new season and purchased what I needed. Her sewing days ended, and it didn't change our lives. But the story is different in countries where sewing can be the difference between providing for your child or depending on an orphanage or relatives to do it. As I struggled with the finicky cabinet sewing machine in my spare bedroom, I thought about how a sewing machine could become a path toward self-sufficiency in a village.

I introduced Afia and Doris to the people who followed our Facebook page, and two friends who sewed offered to sponsor the women through Peter's organization. They would donate money for the supplies and the entry fee, and I would send them updates on the women's progress. We were on our way to making a difference for two women in Ghana. It was a start.

The first year Steffani and I roomed together in college, I would walk into our apartment and find her on the bedroom floor with her sewing machine, stitching costumes for the theater department. It wasn't a hobby, and after finishing her MFA in Costume Design, she moved to Hollywood and worked on the set of television shows, movies, making clothes for A-list actresses. A year before we started the sewing apprenticeships, she had published a book about pattern designing, so I called her as soon as we began talking about helping seamstresses learn the skill and earn income.

"Can you design a pattern for a bag? If the women in our program can learn to sew it, we can sell it here."

"Tell me everything about this," she said as I walked across the grocery store parking lot in Tulsa. "I'm so in."

In three weeks, she designed a bag, sent the prototype and two patterns, and told us that because it was an original design, we were free to name it. We probably could have been more creative, but The Ankaase Bag seemed to fit. It was roomy with four interior pockets, a big outside pocket, and a strap long enough to wear as a crossbody. I hounded everyone about buying one of these bags, and for a while, most of my friends carried an Ankaase bag. Every time we traveled to Ghana, we brought back a suitcase filled with these bags, each one with a piece of paper pinned to the inside with the seamstress's name written in block letters. Not one bag was the same proportion, which was frustrating until I turned the imperfections into a marketing feature.

"They're handmade and not in a factory," I told people,

which meant that no one was buying a product made in a sweatshop-type environment. Most of the time we don't think of the origins of our purchases, or the people who work in an unsafe environment to ensure we can buy cheap clothing and accessories. I did whatever I could to convince people to connect with Ankaase through purchasing "products with a purpose."

We wanted the apprenticeship and student sponsorship programs to have an equal focus, but Peter's heart was with the children. He tried to get excited about sewing, apprenticeships and Ankaase bags, but it was education that kept him dreaming about new possibilities. He wanted to build a school. We didn't. We wanted to expand the program to help women start all kinds of businesses. But he was cautious.

"You can't do it all," he said. "You're going to end up making it complicated."

But Isaac and I knew we could handle both, so we pushed. And Peter pushed back. He was in his 70s and certain about what he wanted to do. He made no apologies for where his vision was leading him. I respected his passion and heart for the families in Ankaase, but it was time to part ways. I thought his lessons in Ghanaian culture and life in the villages had prepared me to forge ahead without making it complicated, but of course, that would prove naïve.

When one story ends, another begins. Isaac and I left Peter's organization, ACEF, at the same time. From that first day he walked into the church to translate the interviews, I knew Isaac and I could work together well. We both wanted to continue helping women find financial stability in Ankaase and nearby rural villages, and we were sure our teamwork could make a difference in Ghana. He would identify the needs of women and at-risk students in Ankaase and nearby villages while I carried the coffee can around my neighborhood, raising money to meet those needs.

There is an African proverb that says, "When you pray, move your feet." I decided, with much trepidation, to move my feet and start a nonprofit. The twitch was back—the one that told me it was time to jump in and fix something, this time on a bigger scale. It was the twitch that scared me because I didn't know the first thing about starting a nonprofit, but everything in me was ready to jump.

BLOG POST, JANUARY 8, 2013

I made a scarf yesterday. It is possibly the ugliest scarf that has ever been stitched anywhere, anytime, anyplace. Yes, the fabric is nice—you can't go wrong with yellow and flowers—however, if you held it in your hands and looked at it closely, you would be sad for me. It's my first sewing project, and I think it's clear I am not a seamstress.

But two ladies In Ghana are on their way to becoming professional seamstresses and yesterday was their first day of apprenticeship at a seamstress shop in Ankaase. And so, I stitched that messy scarf in honor of them. I'm not sure if I'm more excited about the sewing or more charged up to win a victory over the machine. Either way, I'm not giving up. And I'm praying for our seamstress apprentices. For me, sewing is just a whim. I'll make some scarves, maybe convert some t-shirts into shopping bags (found that easy-to-do project from Martha Stewart, go figure). But for our seamstress apprentices, it's an opportunity for a changed life. They're stepping into a career, which for a woman in Ghana is like climbing a steep mountain. Fortunately, our apprentices have lots of climbing support from some other seamstresses who live here in the U.S. Thank you, Diana and Janet, for sponsoring them. I know that by next week, our apprentices will have far surpassed my skill level—in fact, that may have happened today. I'm so happy for them and excited about what the future holds.

And in May, I think I'll take my sorry little scarf to Ghana so the three of us can have a good laugh.

CHAPTER FOUR

Setting in Motion

BLOG POST, DECEMBER 2, 2013

There is a story that makes its way around the Internet about a commencement speech given by Winston Churchill, in which he stood up in front of a graduating class and simply said: "Never give-up. Never give up. Never give up." Then he sat down.

Just so you know, that speech never took place. But I like the story and have claimed it when I needed a dramatic reminder to never give up, never give up, never give up.

He did make a speech in October 1941 at his alma mater, the Harrow School, and said this:

"Never give in, never give in, never, never, never, never-in nothing, great or small, large or petty—never give in except to convictions

of honour and good sense."

He followed this up with other thoughts, but this seems to be the origin of the urban legend speech, which is a very different kind of speech because there is a subtle difference in the wording "in" as opposed to "up." Giving up is quitting something. Giving in is entering into something.

I hate giving up on projects, dreams, plans. But I'm pretty good at giving in to fear, disillusionment, doubt, and a host of other things that might tempt me to give up.

I think the distinction between Churchill's words is important. We first give in to something before we give up on something. I find myself in the danger zone these days as the setbacks come in clusters. There were several this week and I spent the day yesterday wondering if I was crazy, had jumped the gun or taken the wrong path. Things seemed to be on the verge of falling apart, and I went through a list of possible reasons. I cried, cleaned my house, and thought about applying for a job at the newspaper where I used to work. The clincher came earlier that morning when I heard the news that Isaac was sick in a hospital bed in Ghana. As I mopped my kitchen floor in a panic, I blamed myself —certain that he had been working too hard. And of course, that was my fault. My temptations to give in continued all day and into the evening. This morning I woke up to the news that this coming Thursday, the day of my party to raise money for apprentices and students, the high temperature will be 26 degrees, accompanied by sleet and possible snow. Of course, the weather is beautiful all week until that day, when it turns into winter again. I already felt like the girl who threw a party, and no one came. I feared the worst and doubted my crazy ideas.

And then, I thought about Churchill's speech—the real one. "Never give in. Never. Never. Never."

I ran across this quote from Francis Chan a little later: "When it's hard and you are doubtful, give more."

Today, Isaac is better and will deliver beds and bed nets to families before the week is over. I changed the date of my party and crossed my fingers about the weather, then put a big pot of pinto beans on the stove (comfort food). Things are definitely not on the verge of falling apart. I was just on the verge of giving in to my fears, worries and doubts. And according to Churchill, who my father-in-law thought a genius, I should never do this.

I'm digging my heels in—deep.

I spent the last two weeks of July 2013 in the Colorado mountains with spiral notebooks scattered across the table of our vacation condo. There was a notebook for nonprofit financial structure, one dedicated to ideas for the organization's name, and one that I kept private because it contained all the fears that kept surfacing in between moments of certainty. While we hiked, my mind churned with ideas about how to best communicate the needs and our mission, and how little I knew about running a nonprofit. Isaac was also messaging me every day with stories of families who needed help, and that kept my fears in the background. We would figure out along the way what we didn't already know. I was constantly counting forward five hours to Ghana time, and then I would think about the heat and humidity while I felt the cool, dry mountain air on my skin.

For decades, we traveled to the same area of Colorado every summer with my parents, and when my mother died in 2008, Dad continued to come with us. He would join us on a few hikes, but what he loved most was staring at Pagosa Peak from the condo's back deck. I had set up a work area on the deck, which meant he watched me scribble in my notebooks every morning and afternoon as we sat at the table together. During our two weeks in Colorado, he never asked me about it until the last day, when I was staring at my laptop screen, checking on the availability of a website domain name.

"What is it you've been doing on this vacation?" He laid his thick paperback on the table and pointed at my notebooks. "You're all wound up."

"I'm starting a nonprofit."

He stared at the mountain, and we sat in silence together for a while.

"So I'll have to keep asking people for money." Neither one of us brought up the neighborhood coffee can fundraiser, but he smiled a little. I looked at the old straw hat he was wearing and the deep lines on his face. Dad would turn 80 the next year, and I knew he could never travel to Ghana, but I think he got it. He was a generous man with an obsession to fix things that weren't quite right. He would tinker on a repair for hours and most of the time he was successful, but sometimes he made things worse, and drove himself a little crazy. We had that in common.

The domain name was available, and I clicked the link to purchase it.

"Rising Village," I said to Dad. "That's the name of our nonprofit."

"Sounds good to me," he replied. I settled back into my chair and joined him in staring at the mountains, doing my best to not appear wound up.

What you don't learn in school, you can find on the Internet.

I discovered a plethora of websites, forums, online courses, and blogs dedicated to forming a nonprofit. My husband, Kyle was a nonprofit director, but he had never formed one, and so I immersed myself in learning how it's done. When we got back to Tulsa, I spent hours in my home office, winding down my work with the magazine and preparing to launch Rising Village. I'll still write, I told myself as I packed up the back issues of our magazine and transformed my office from editor to director.

Three other women and I started our magazine, *Mia*, and I loved the collaboration and creative energy around working with a team. As I was barricaded in my office, learning what makes some nonprofits work and others fail, I realized that the team aspect was missing. When you are going solo, lots of fearful interior voices pop up at random moments and shout about risk and failure. I needed some outside voices to shout back, so I got busy and assembled a small board of directors made up of friends who were also looking for opportunities to jump in and make a difference.

Once a board was in place, I taught myself how to build a website (which produced expletives and desk-pounding) and started a spreadsheet with a list of possible donors who would give monthly. I had learned about the need for small nonprofits to secure recurring donations, so I included this in our financial plan. Isaac applied for NGO status in Ghana because scribbled in one of my Colorado notebooks, underlined and circled, were the words, *Must have Ghana staff*. I wanted everything in place that would ensure we could transfer the work completely over to Ghanaians at some future time.

While Isaac was busy looking for another person to join him in the Ghana work, I pulled my son, Colin, into the U.S. work.

He had just graduated college with a degree in communications, so he agreed to handle our social media and strategize ways to expand our networks. In October, Colin and I drove to Oklahoma City to file our certificate of incorporation in person at the Secretary of State office. This was the first step in receiving our nonprofit status from the Internal Revenue Service. We could have mailed it, but we wanted a road trip and an excuse to celebrate at a West African restaurant, Mama Sinmi's Chop House. Over goat soup and red red, Colin and I made plans to travel to Ghana in January to meet the Rising Village families and our new staff.

In the meantime, Kyle and I worked on the long application for 501(c)(3) status and prepared to wait. In late 2013, the process hadn't yet been streamlined, and applications could take up to six months to be approved. That timeline would be longer if the application was incomplete or the IRS had follow-up questions. We could still receive donations during the waiting period but were prohibited from setting up a process for our recurring donations, so we treated our application like a life or death document. I mailed the thick packet off in December, and it felt like a Christmas gift to have it out of my hands.

Two siblings, Max and Mena, would be the first students in our education sponsorship program. They lived with their grandmother and had been in and out of schools for several years. It was time for them to have reliable school fees and stability. Because of her gender, Mena was the sibling who missed the most school. Often, it is the females who lose out when there is money for only one or two children in a family to attend school. Max was enrolled in school and able to attend more often than Mena, although neither of them had steady attendance.

At the time they entered our sponsorship program, Mena spent her days cooking and cleaning for the family. The first photo I received of her showed a thin, barefoot girl sitting on a low wooden bench, grinding peppers with a hand carved pestle. Like most young girls in Ghana, her hair was buzzed to the scalp, which made me focus on her face. Isaac stood behind her taking the photo, and she had turned her head to smile at him. Her eyes were bright and wide, and her smile was confident. Isaac never took a photo that made a person look hopeless because they weren't. The children and women in our programs were capable and smart, and we didn't ask them to look sad or needy in photos. There was enough emotional manipulation in the world of charity organizations and nonprofits, and I was gaining a heightened sensitivity to the "white savior" complex.

My faith culture believed deeply in sharing love and resources with the world. My own church had been a crucial support as we started Rising Village, the first to give funds, tell their friends, and fill positions on our board of directors. I was also reading and researching the history of colonialism. Westerners had historically believed it would strengthen a country's economic power and used it as a necessary form of civilizing and proselytizing. For centuries, colonizers landed on shores to bring "good news", often accompanied by claims that traditional culture was depraved and needed salvation. Colonialism in Africa ended in the mid-70s, but there were still many ways white people left a heavy footprint alongside their good intentions. It is easy to presume that our personal religions and customs are the answer to the world's problems, and if only people would adapt to our way of life, their smiles would return.

That sentence I had underlined and circled, *Must have Ghana staff*, meant Isaac was front and center, because he knew best how to help the people in his village. We couldn't leave behind the work with students, but we wanted to address the problem at the starting point—the struggle so many mothers faced in finding stable income and financial stability. We were scraping together resources, and I begged Isaac to keep the focus on income sustainability for single mothers and school fees for children. He agreed, and then a month later he messaged me about bed nets and sent a photograph of a young boy lying on a floor mat, sick with malaria. Malarial symptoms were common because many people slept under old bed nets that were filled with holes. "They don't realize that the holes in their nets are causing their sickness," he told me. "And they shouldn't be sleeping on the floor. We need to provide them with bedding, nets and education about malaria."

Isaac and I were looking at the needs from different vantage points. News was spreading in the village about the new NGO and people were coming to his house at all hours to ask for help. He was discovering needs he had never known existed in his village. Isaac hated to turn people away, but it was clear that even if we kept our focus on single mothers and vulnerable children, they would need to be healthy to attend school and work their apprenticeships. I was in the U.S., remembering the computer lab and trying to make sure we didn't make promises we couldn't keep.

"There are so many needs," he said. "When you come, you'll see."

A few weeks later, I opened Facebook and saw a post from Isaac. It was a photo of him in the hospital with a small paragraph that said he was feeling better and hoped to be home soon. I immediately sent him a message asking what had happened. He wrote back, "malarial symptoms."

This threw me into a guilty panic about how hard he had been working, but it also convinced me we should fund bed nets and bedding for the Rising Village families. Ghana seemed far away, and I felt helpless. We needed to hire more staff to work alongside Isaac, so when he recovered, we both agreed it was time to look for someone to assist him.

Meanwhile, in the U.S., I had been planning our first fund-raising event. We called it Shopfest, and we were going to sell Ankaase bags, Krobo bead bracelets, Rising Village t-shirts, and gift cards to fund specific needs. I invited everyone I knew and asked them to bring a friend. Over the years, as needs continued to grow and our inventory of handmade items expanded, these shopping events would turn into something bigger than I could have imagined. But this first one was for Regina, our newest seamstress apprentice, the students Mena and Max, and three women who needed funds for a start-up business. Despite having to change the date because Oklahoma weather is unpredictable, Shopfest raised all the money we needed to provide their skills training, business start-up funds, bedding and education for the year.

"How easy was that?" I asked Kyle at the end of the evening.

Maybe "easy" wasn't the right word but selling gave me an adrenaline rush. I loved the challenge of seeing people buy products and knowing how far that money could go to help the families. The proceeds from one bag would send a kid to school for a semester. Twelve bracelets funded an apprentice for three years. Two t-shirts were enough for a mattress. I learned to connect the need with the product, which gave people a two for one good feeling: retail therapy and charitable contribution.

In January, Colin and I packed flashcards, extension cords, conversation hearts, cheese, and onesies. We always carried an interesting combination of items to Ghana. It happened the same way every time: we would arrange everything in the suitcase, balance it on the luggage scale, then redistribute the items between the suitcases to make sure we weren't over the fifty-pound limit. We packed to the weight limit, so if the scale was off by a pound, we would have to offload things at the airport. During packing week, I became overly dramatic, sweating and stressing until the suitcases were one pound underweight and threatening anyone who touched them. By the time we had hauled our luggage to the airport and checked in, everything felt surreal, like I was stepping out of one atmosphere and into another. From my cramped seat on British Airways, Delta, or whoever had the cheapest airfare, I would watch the flight path on the navigation screen, awed that I could travel across the ocean and then walk the red dirt roads on another continent.

On our first official Rising Village trip, Colin and I spent eight days meeting the families who were now in our program. Isaac was right about seeing the needs up close. Reading his messages about the people who came to his house at all hours and seeing the photos had kept me connected, but sitting in their homes and listening to their stories drew me deeper into their lives. Many people lived one day away from pulling their children from school or handing them over to relatives. I couldn't imagine living with that kind of uncertainty when it came to my children. As a young mother, I had stressed about their school attendance and other things that might make life difficult for them. But I could always walk into a market and buy them enough food for a week and assure them they would always sleep under our roof, safe with their dad and me. Anything less for my children was unacceptable, so it had to be unacceptable for everybody else's children. Isaac and I had many discussions at the dinner table in Ghana about why some people believe there are cultures who value their children less than others. It isn't true, but that wrong belief often gives us permission to look away from the suffering and ignore the inequities. In the eyes of every mother and grandparent in Ghana, I saw deep love for the children.

On our last day in Ankaase, we welcomed James into our program, an eleven-year-old whose parents had died several years earlier. He was living with relatives, his bed wedged into a storage room corner at the back of a house. When we met with his family and provided "news from the road," we told them we had found a sponsor in the U.S. who would cover James' school fees for the entire year. His grandmother stood up and bent over to take my hands, tears streaming down her weathered cheeks as she thanked me.

"I'm only here to deliver the news," I said to her. "Your grandson's sponsor is Carol, and Beth provided his uniform. I'm going to tell them how grateful you are." Isaac translated, and she nodded. "And Isaac found James and enrolled him in school." I pointed at Isaac, and she grabbed his hands as she continued to repeat, "medaase, medaase."

James sat on the dirt behind his grandmother, his new backpack balanced on his lap, watching me curiously. On every trip, there were moments when I wondered if I should be somewhere else, maybe at home, minding my business. I felt like an intruder, intent on digging my heels into a place I could never fully comprehend, hoping to make sense of the world's chaos by fixing one small thing, and then one more.

Maybe that's the way we all stay sane, or at least avoid losing hope.

BLOG POST, JANUARY 31, 2014

Tonight, we finished our groundnut soup and rice ball and have been sitting in the living area and singing along to hymns on Eunice's cell phone. The singer is Sonnie Badu, who I did not know before tonight. It's amazing that I am singing the same hymns with my Ghanaian friends I grew up singing in my grandmother's church. They sing much better than I do, by the way. But get this: my friends also love Dolly Parton, Jimmy Reeves, and Kenny Rogers. Surprise! Eunice has "Coat of Many Colors" on her cell phone. This has completely made my night and not just because I love Dolly Parton, but because it reminds me of how small the world is. We've talked about everything from Illuminati to Snoop Dog. We don't understand either, by the way.

So tomorrow we're walking to Kofi and Agnes's little house to meet their family and see the new baby (#8!). Then we'll climb into the back of a motor tricycle and travel to Kofi's farm where, thanks to donors, he will begin planting cocoa after the dry season. Agnes will begin her Puff bread business after she is back on her feet, in about a month.

The rain has brought a cool breeze that is making the curtains flutter just the slightest bit. I have old hymns running through my head and friends surrounding me. I'm a little homesick, so I am grateful for these blessings. It's been a very good day.

Until tomorrow, good night from Ankaase.

CHAPTER FIVE

The Way Forward

BLOG POST DRAFT, SEPTEMBER 5, 2014

"A religion that professes to be concerned with the souls of men and is not concerned with the slums that damn them, the economic conditions that strangle them, and the social conditions that cripple them is a dry-as-dust religion," said Martin Luther King, Jr.

I'm on a learning curve these days, reading everything from World Bank development books to William Easterly to articles about the effects of European colonization. My head is spinning. When I began working in Ghana, I decided it would never be enough to simply know the need. I wanted to understand, as best I could, the how and why of poverty in that particular place. And, as it turns out, it's complicated. Many are the times I have tossed aside the weighty tomes and kicked back with a good Grisham novel. But then something draws me back to plodding through dense books and articles to understand the why and the how. Suddenly I'm back to highlighting and reading a sentence four times to barely understand it.

When I read the above quote recently, I realized why I've been agonizing over this stuff. I've clocked hours on mission trips to far-flung places, counted the hands raised and the souls saved, only to return and give the people we left hardly a thought once the high wore off. And I've had that little prick of doubt that makes me wonder if some of those numbers we were proud to announce back home were people responding to something besides the nudge of the Holy Spirit. Perhaps they were nudged by the hope that we might help them escape from the stranglehold of poverty. I don't know. Just tossing around thoughts here.

Ghana is the Bible belt of West Africa. Even a village the size of Ankaase has four churches, one on almost every corner, and Christian symbolism is everywhere. Businesses get in on this by choosing names that reflect the religious culture: Nearer My God Construction Company. Lord's Winners Investment Services. In Thee Hotel (my favorite). We noticed a decorative symbol called *Gye Nyame*, on clothing, jewelry, wood carvings, even the plastic chairs we sat in for our "news from the road" meetings. *Gye Nyame* means, "except for God," and symbolizes God's omnipotence. Nothing is to be feared, many Ghanaians believe, except God.

I hedged my answer when people in the U.S. asked if we were sharing the gospel. I would resort to pithy responses like, "We're trying to leave it better than we found it," or "We want to share love through action." A few people thought we should make converts, which gave me angst. I dumped many of my blog posts into the draft folder as I worked through my misgivings about evangelistic endeavors in impoverished places. I knew of organizations and mission groups that swooped in and out of the poorest countries with suitcases filled with backpacks, Bibles, and an agenda to bring home a report on the number of converted souls. We took backpacks and Bibles also, but we couldn't get on board with the soul-saving agenda. Ghanaians aren't on board with it either.

The country has a large Muslim population in the northern regions and Christianity is the major religion in the south. There is overlap between the two populations in many areas, but neither religion believes in converting the other. Thank God. Ghanaians like peace, and they know that if one religion decides the other should adopt their brand of salvation, it will not turn out well. They've seen the tumultuous result of a strained relationship between the two religions in other African countries.

Too many of us mission trip participants never bothered to understand the history and nuances of spiritual culture in the places we visited, assuming that "sharing the gospel" works the same everywhere. But Ghanaians are gracious hosts, so they will welcome groups from Western countries who arrive laden with t-shirts and craft supplies for Vacation Bible Schools. In the part of Ghana where we worked, children have been in church since their naming ceremony, ten days after they were born. If you want to have a spiritual conversation with a Ghanaian, they will jump in and pepper it with a few Bible verses, bits of sermons, and the chorus of a hymn. Churches in Ghana hold revivals, summer camps, youth conferences, women's Bible studies, and Christian concerts.

When I took my friend, Shannon, over with us in June 2014, we visited the home of a young woman, Francisca, who wanted to become a seamstress apprentice. She and several relatives were sleeping on a bed frame without a mattress and only two thin blankets between the wood slats and their backs. As Francisca walked with us to the guesthouse, Shannon talked about her mother back in Phoenix, who was ill with Parkinson's disease. I could tell that my friend didn't want to share her own struggles after seeing the living conditions at Francisca's house, but Ghanaians always ask about family and Francisca wanted to know everything. It had been a hard trip for Shannon. She was worried about her mother and at one point, Francisca linked her arm in Shannon's and began singing an old hymn we both remembered from childhood. Shannon joined her, and together they sang two verses of that hymn in English. No one was bringing the people in Ghana revelations about a God they hadn't already heard about. That happened six centuries earlier when European colonizers and missionaries landed on the Gold Coast, and from there, the missionary activity never ceased. The village of Ankaase and the entire southern half of the country were soaked in Christianity.

I'm no good at telling people how to get to heaven, but I can get behind the idea of saving someone from hell on earth.

We returned, and I immediately began dragging Colin around to speaking events where we would unpack our wares like itinerant peddlers and set up a shop somewhere in the room. My presentation started with, "I don't sew. But somehow I've ended up in a place where a sewing machine can feed a family." On the screen behind me was a photo of the mother and baby girl

Peter and I met in the orphanage, a profile of them looking into each other's eyes. She had wanted me to photograph the two of them and send it to Peter in case she left her daughter that day. I wanted everyone in the room to understand the hell of having to walk your child into an orphanage because you can't afford food, clothes, and school fees. I explained that in the rural villages, if you are a woman, most banks won't consider giving you credit to start a business. And if you are a single and poor woman, with no family to help, you have almost no access to the skills training that might save you from the dead-end of petty trading. I would continue to talk while I scrolled through photos of the women and children, watching faces to see if we were connecting. When I finished the presentation, I pointed to the shop we had set up in a corner of the room and told people that buying products can make a difference for a woman. The funky fabric of the Ankaase bags drew shoppers to the table, where they could also purchase batik fabric aprons, jewelry, children's skirts, t-shirts, and headbands. We scattered framed photos of the women in Ghana between the products.

I would end with a plea for everyone to "purchase for a purpose." The seamstresses would receive all the income from their sold products, and the proceeds from the jewelry went toward supplementing the salaries and expenses of our staff in Ghana. My presentation skipped the part about salaries and expenses because most people don't want to hear what part of their money goes for the sim card and car petrol. It feels better to know that the money is funneled directly to the mother holding her newborn baby, or the little girl in the yellow school uniform dress. But Isaac had to fill his car with gas to get from one village to another and add more sim card data so staff on both continents could hold Facetime meetings. I left that part out. Instead, I told everyone that buying a recycled glass bead bracelet would fund six weeks of school or pay for an apprentice's sewing chair. I kept silent about the need for overhead costs so I wouldn't lose my audience.

We spoke mostly at churches because, for decades, my roots were buried deep in those places. Despite the criticism of organized religion, I've watched how church people mobilize to meet a need. They will plan a fundraiser, take up a collection, gather a work team and get rolling. Churches often disagree about what makes the world a better place, some leaning toward personal morals, others toward societal justice, but we tried to be clear about what we were doing. Our mission was to "transform villages through family preservation," which I had first written in one of those Colorado notebooks. It was lofty, and the last two words a little vague. Family preservation could mean a hundred different things depending on how you define the words *family* and *preservation*. Our goal was to keep children out of the orphanage or the hands of traffickers, and in the arms of their mothers or family caregivers. That was a clearer statement, but too bulky for nonprofit marketing materials. And we knew it was hard to disagree with the desire to keep families together.

We provided Isaac with a good camera and directed him to keep taking and sending photos.

During that first year, he wrote "Thank You for Giving" on a piece of cardboard and gave it to one child in the family to hold up for photos. After a while, the cardboard was bent and torn along one edge. "We don't need the cardboard sign anymore," I told him, and he seemed relieved.

Nonprofits learn how to market their mission. And sometimes that involves putting people's needs on display, splashing them across social media along with photos and stories so we can help make life better for them. I preferred raising money with success stories, rather than playing on sympathies, but that assumes there are enough success stories to tell. For the sake of the people and the organization, our programs needed to make a real difference and produce lasting change.

At our events, everyone had a Krobo bead in their chair or on the table in front of them as a reminder that discarded glass can be transformed into a magnificent bead. People who feel crushed can rise. The ugliest situation can transform into an inspiring story. No one is on a hopeless journey. I could churn out a dozen inspiring phrases that served the metaphor, but sometimes, the words gloss over the complicated lives of people, and convince us that change is linear. It's not.

Puff bread, also called *bofrot*, is like a deep-fried donut, but without the sugar. In Ghana, women fry the bread over a cooking fire, then load it into a warming cart and "set up shop" near a busy road. Agnes wanted to start one of these businesses, and she was certain she could make it work.

Not every woman wanted to sew, and some had ideas for other types of businesses they wanted to start. We agreed that we should think big, and how hard could it be to help a woman start a small business?

Colin and I visited Agnes on that third trip to Ghana and met her seven children in front of their home, a one room structure on a hill outside the village. Isaac had already entered her into the Income Generation program and a sponsor in Tulsa gave money for her business start-up. We were all excited about puff bread. Agnes was hanging out laundry when I arrived—lots of cloth baby diapers on a clothesline in her dirt yard. Her five daughters were busy doing various chores, and one of them had her 18-month-old brother strapped on her back while she worked in the outdoor kitchen. While we talked through a translator, Agnes would stop to answer questions from her daughters, or attend to the newest family member, an infant girl who was napping fretfully on a bed inside the room. We talked about the family's need for more income, and she expressed excitement about earning money.

Three months later, when Agnes began her puff bread business, we had big plans for her. She couldn't afford the warming cart yet, but that would come, along with a business name, signage, maybe an apron with a clever logo. We were even dreaming of a storefront someday where she could sell bakery items. Agnes was on board with all our big ideas, and when we visited in November, we planned to be her most faithful puff bread customers. But she was only there for two days, because her children were sick, or she needed to gather food for their evening meal, or there were too many chores to be done at home now that the girls were in school.

"She's still learning how to be a businesswoman," Isaac said. "We will give her more time and see what happens." The sponsor in the U.S. who provided the start-up funds had a donut food truck and sent us with a "Lick Your Lips Mini-Donuts" t-shirt as a gift for Agnes. It was a great story, and we were still hopeful, but later that fall, Agnes quit her Puff bread business. The family, especially the two babies, needed her at home.

I was heartbroken and asked Isaac what else we could do for her.

"We can't do anything else," he said. "We did our best, and she knows that, so let's just pray God will show her the way forward."

What way forward was there for her now? I didn't feel like we had done our best for Agnes, and I had not come to Ghana expecting to fail. Success, defined as whatever predetermined outcome we set forth, was the goal. That might have been part of the problem, since all the big ideas and dreams were ours, not hers. We had flown faster and further than Agnes, not realizing her family obligations would make starting a business complicated. We hadn't counted on taking the long-view and digging in to help her work through the complications so she could keep going. I worried about Agnes and her children, so we continued to fund their school fees until she could find a source of income that worked for her. I reminded myself we had provided them with bedding and nets, so we had done some good, but it felt like a defeat for her, and us.

No one in the nonprofit world likes to talk about failure. When Agnes dropped out of the program, I didn't announce it, but sent out a slick annual report with colorful stories about our successes. Regina was thriving in her seamstress apprenticeship, and we were selling her children's clothing in the U.S., along with other items she stitched. Emmanuel, 17-years-old and absent from school for three years, caught up quickly and had won a district-wide speech contest for high school students. Donors provided Abigail with a bicycle so she and her baby, Florence, didn't wilt in the sun for five miles as they trekked from her village to the seamstress shop.

I included numbers in the report to show how many people were benefiting from our programs. The numbers included funds we had raised, items sold, money earned by apprentices, and the growing staff in Ghana. But an annual report rarely tells a story in the way it really happened, and the successes look small when they are in print. An annual report is a tool that attempts to present the most positive image of a nonprofit, and Agnes's story just didn't fit. Also, comparison is a sneaky thief, and it was tempting to measure our work by looking at what other nonprofits in Ghana and elsewhere were doing, especially the ones who landed in the country with large-scale plans.

I worried about everything during that first year—keeping donors satisfied, not overworking our staff, living up to the promises we made to families. I wanted to do everything in Ghana with a level of perfection that doesn't exist in cross-cultural work (or anywhere else). It was heartbreaking to say goodbye to Agnes, and to admit we weren't equipped to help women start businesses from scratch. I fretted about what other people, especially her sponsor, would think.

"We did our best," I told the sponsor. "But it wasn't enough." I didn't have a cheery, hopeful sentence to wrap up Agnes's story. Life is hard for women in Ghana, and our efforts weren't going to always lead us in straightforward steps that produced happy endings. We would continue to see Agnes's family during our next few visits to Ghana, and then she started another small business selling eggs. We eventually lost touch. You tell the dramatic, happy-ending stories at the big event, but other stories you tell in smaller circles, when you're talking about how life doesn't always follow a straight line, and there isn't a tidy ending.

Here's another one.

Mena, our first sponsored student, got pregnant just as the

school year began in 2014. Isaac informed me in a very formal Facebook message, and I wrote back two panicked paragraphs that ended with, "I can't EVEN IMAGINE how this happened!" Then I deleted it all and simply said, "Okay, thank you for letting me know."

My church sponsored both Mena and her brother Max, and I was wringing my hands about how to tell them. I didn't need to worry. In June, a week after she gave birth to a son, a minister and several members of our church traveled to Ghana with me, their suitcases filled with baby items from people in the congregation and the staff. They gave her a baby shower, passed her infant son around, and told Mena that she was going to be a wonderful mother.

My angst about everything we did in Ghana has always run parallel to the truth that control is an illusion, especially when you are 6,000 miles away. I was learning to let go of perfection, glossy annual reports that only tell half the story, and the expectations of people who didn't understand the culture—and that included me.

The church folks were okay with the messy part of Mena's story, embracing it as part of the nonlinear journey we're all on. This helped silence the cynic in me, and I counted it as a beautiful success story.

BLOG POST, NOV 16, 2014

Each day that passes, I realize with startling clarity that I am not saving the world. Sometimes let's-save-the-world and change-the-world can be effective rally cries if you find the proper audience, but it can also be a dangerous mentality. As we entered each village where we work in Ghana, I once again reminded myself I have far more to learn than teach, far more to absorb than dispense. And on this trip, I tried to clear my vision and see what was in front of me. Unfortunately, we Westerners glide into different parts of Africa with too many opinions, ideas, images, and solutions blocking our vision. We think we know how it should be, and so we come ready to fix things and save people. I only know this because that's me: fixing and saving.

But that's all wrong. I can't fix my own life, so I'm not sure why I think I can do this for anyone else. I want to connect with our friends in Ghana by walking gently, in a way that allows me to see and learn. If I strip away what I think I know about the people in Ghana—or anywhere in the world—this might be possible.

So over the past four days—starting with the 36-hour airport/airline festivities—I've been closing my eyes and seeing, once again, all that we were privileged to see in Ghana. I've been reliving moments and asking myself what I have learned from them. I've been dragging my vision across the landscape of a village, a mud and thatch house, a dark room, a contagious smile, and a hand-crank sewing machine. What does it mean that this is one young woman's life day in and day out? Maybe it means nothing. Or maybe it holds answers to questions I ask every day.

CHAPTER SIX

Space

BLOG POST DRAFT, DECEMBER 18, 2014

My job is like this: Some days I travel to Ghana, and other days I iron wax fabric aprons in my office. I did the latter today, with a table-top ironing board positioned next to the printer. It was a collision of sounds—the printer humming while the iron belched steam. Hovered over my desk like a workplace domestic goddess, I learned two things: 1) tabletop ironing boards are mostly useless but will eventually work if you're patient and don't mind the board sliding across the desk every time you move the iron. And 2) even the most mundane task can be done with passion if you remember your purpose. So, what is the purpose of ironing wax fabric aprons on a tabletop ironing board in my office? This: To help at-risk women rise from the dead-end cycle of poverty and earn an income that gives them dignity and hope so they can be the mothers they want to be.

Oh, and because I want to sell the aprons.

So, we have a little something you can do. You can buy stuff. You're probably already doing it anyway, right?

Buying stuff for a good cause is not a new concept. And, I don't like to knock off great ideas; I like to generate new ones. But sometimes great ideas are great for a reason, which is why I'm selling stuff. And I'm asking you to buy it so that mothers like Abigail can provide for their babies. This young mother is an apprentice in Ghana who walks an hour each way from her village of Dumakyi to Ankaase so she can apprentice under a professional seamstress. She will do this for two more years, during which time she will earn no income. Essentially, she is in school. But she has a beautiful baby named Florence, and Abigail needs the dignity of earning income while she is learning her craft so she can care for her. Regina, who is also a Rising Village seamstress apprentice, has the same story—only her daughter is Betty. Regina is creative, smart, and courageous. These women don't need a handout. They need an opportunity to sell what they make, but they can't do it in Ghana quite yet. So, we're selling beautiful children's clothing that these two apprentices have stitched. And we're selling other wax fabric items from these apprentices and other seamstresses in the village so we can continue to bring more women into the program. We pay each woman we work with a fair wage, and we provide them with the wax fabric (purchased locally) to stitch the items. They work in a shop with lots of laughter, chatter, babies nearby—sometimes strapped to their backs—and arms pumping as they stitch on hand crank sewing machines. We build a relationship with each one of the seamstresses and apprentices because we can't imagine doing it any other way. These are special women who are working hard to make life better for their children in a place where the odds are stacked against them.

Does buying children's clothing, or table runners, or fabric neck-laces from a few seamstress apprentices in Ghana make the world a better place? I don't know.

But I'm ready to find out.

By April 2014, our family's dining room table no longer functioned as an eating space. It was covered in African beads, jewelry making supplies, batik fabric bags, aprons, skirts, children's clothing, product tags, and photos. I was traveling back and forth to Ghana twice a year to visit our four staff, six apprentices and twelve sponsored students. And when I was back in Tulsa, I hounded everyone in my line of vision to buy stuff, give money, sponsor an apprentice or student, or help fund our trips to Ghana. No person or place escaped the cause.

Our house fell victim to my frantic need to sell the products. What had been our personal space of retreat was now a public venue for frequent pop-up shops, and our home address the pick-up location for products purchased through Rising Village's online store. I hauled a long folding table into the house and set it up beside the overloaded dining room table, then enticed our youngest daughter, Alison, to make hoop earrings and tie knots on Krobo bead stretch bracelets. Colin was still handling his Rising Village duties from the spare bedroom, and when Erin announced she would move to an apartment, I quickly claimed her room for the nonprofit's office space.

No one complained, but the walls were closing in. We didn't invite people over for dinner or get-togethers as often because it required a day to pack and hide the world of Rising Village. My family needed their house back, so I added "office space" to the list of things I asked donors for and started begging for help by showing photos of the mess in my house. After only a few weeks, I got a message from the doctor who pulled our kids' wisdom teeth.

"I know a guy," he said. "He runs a nonprofit also, so he understands."

The guy was Jerry, and the office was his nonprofit baseball training facility. For $100 a month and nothing in writing, he gave us keys to two offices, a small storage room, and a back lobby area to display our products. When we walked into our new space each day, we passed life-size images of famous baseball players and motivational sports posters, but something about this symbiotic relationship between two very different nonprofits made sense. Jerry talked to us about baseball and the Dominican Republic, and we taught him about wax fabric and apprenticeship in Ghana. Some men who worked out at Jerry's facility during the lunch hour bought Regina and Abigail's dresses for their daughters, and the recycled glass bead jewelry for their wives. They would shop, sweat dripping from their foreheads, slugging Gatorade and nodding along to my overly detailed explanations of wax fabric creation.

"They dip wood blocks with symbols on them in hot wax, press it on the fabric, and then dye it in various colors," I told them. "Everywhere the wax is, the dye can't saturate, which leaves blank areas. They repeat the process until they have these multicolored designs. It's very cool."

With a semi-glazed look in their eyes, the guys would politely ask "How much?" hoping to move past the fabric art lesson. I would answer and, while closing the sale, tell them about the women who benefitted from their purchases.

Most of the men who were shopping didn't care much about the wax resist process, but I wanted them to know their purchase helped Regina, Abigail, and eventually seventeen more women who went through our Income Generation program. I was confident in my pitch about how the purchases were making a big difference, and then I learned Regina had taken on a second job.

The apprentices were worried about money. They worked at their shops and salons six days a week, which put an end to the side jobs they strung together for income before entering the program. Regina had gone back to petty trading, selling trinkets like cheap plastic jewelry and blingy hair accessories. Instead of saving money to open a business after her seamstress apprenticeship, she was investing her small income in a side hustle. Isaac sent a photo of her crouched beside her enormous basket of inventory, each small product wrapped in plastic, purchased from a wholesaler who sold to petty traders. I studied her face in the photo and looked for signs of desperation. Her daughter, Betty, was in nursery school during the day, which cost money. Regina had been one of the women we interviewed in the sweltering church building the day I met Isaac and before we began Rising Village. We had not chosen her for the ACEF program that day, but when we started Rising Village, she walked to Isaac's house and asked if we would give her a second chance and fund her apprenticeship entrance. Regina was stubbornly determined to be a good provider for Betty, apparently even if it meant adding a petty trading side hustle.

I wrote a post on the Rising Village blog about Regina's entrepreneurial spirit, and how she had invested some of the income from selling her stitched items to start the side business. I spun it as a success story, but it wasn't. Carting around a basket of plastic-wrapped junk to sell for Betty's nursery school fees wasn't what we envisioned for Regina when she entered the program. It felt like we were failing in our promises to the women, so I decided we would work harder to sell more of their products each month. I needed help with this, so we found two interns, Kelsey and Maddy, who had fresh energy and youthful determination to make a difference.

Colin was growing uncomfortable with the selling and fundraising, so he started hunting for a job that didn't have the word "nonprofit" in its description. He was ready for a monthly paycheck and no more fundraising events, and after landing a job with benefits and paid vacation, he moved on. There were days when I wanted to do the same. Before we launched Rising Village, I did six months of research about the world of nonprofits, including talking to others who were doing similar work. "You'll hate it, and you'll love it," one nonprofit director said, and added, "usually both at the same time."

On the days when I heard from Isaac that a student had dropped out, or an apprentice was not making enough from the sales of her products here in the U.S., it felt like we had stepped into something we didn't fully understand and weren't equipped to carry forward. Americans like quick solutions. Most of us prefer meeting needs that are easily explained and fixed in one or two quick steps. Gratification without the wait. I wanted our big idea of selling the apprentices' products to give measurable results in time for the annual report, or the next social media post, or before someone asked if we were "making progress in Ghana."

"Is this model working for the women?" I would impatiently ask Isaac, and sometimes he would answer yes. But other times, the women had a medical issue or needed medicine for a sick child, and the income from their product sales wasn't enough. Finally, Isaac asked that we give the women a small monthly stipend to help with emergencies.

"Like a salary for sewing the products," he said.

"We want them to have dignity," I told him. We had talked about avoiding models of dependency, and how giving handouts is much easier than finding avenues that lead to long-term self-sufficiency.

"Yes," he wrote back. "We want dignity for them, but we also want them to survive."

I had wrangled everyone in my immediate family into the work of Rising Village, some more than others. From the outside, it seemed that my kids and husband were deeply invested, but that was mostly because I begged for help. Kyle was busy directing his own nonprofit, but his turn was coming.

In the fall of 2015, I bought a journal with the words "What If?" on the cover. I needed a place to write the beginnings of an idea so I could read it back and decide if it was crazy. And then decide if we should do it anyway. I proudly showed the journal to Kyle.

"Isn't that a brilliant cover?" I asked him, waving the journal around. He avoided eye contact. Every next step of Rising Village started with those two words, which usually meant I was about to get wound up and drag the people closest to me into a new project. He had to know he was next on the list.

"What if we opened a small shop?" I asked.

It was the only idea in my journal because it was the only idea that made sense. We could do more for the women if we scaled up our selling of the dresses, bags, aprons, headbands, and jewelry. Maybe add other handmade products that were low-cost inventory. I was sure we could raise the funds needed to cover the shop's lease and other overhead costs. It was the board's job to make sure I wasn't pitching a great idea without a solid plan for its success, which was exactly what I was doing.

I once tried to write a five-year plan, which seemed more like coming up with a version of what *could* happen, depending on what I thought *might* happen. It was speculation, with no idea what obstacles and opportunities might show up on the path. Eventually, I buried the long-range plan in a folder on my computer and never opened it again. Our failure with Agnes had taught me it might be better to sketch possibilities, expect that real life might derail them, and reroute when necessary. None of that fits my personality, but it kept me from feeling surprised when things didn't follow a straight line.

I prepared an energetic pitch to the board filled with a list of good reasons a shop was the right next step. I was going for passion instead of a business plan.

"We need to move to the next level." (Cliches were not beyond me.)

"If we don't try this, we'll always wonder if it might have worked."

"There's no shop like this in Tulsa."

"We need to connect with our own community."

And my final and most persuasive argument is the one that will always be true.

"You can't feel guilty about shopping when you know someone else is benefitting from your purchase." That seemed like a good business plan.

The vote was unanimous in favor of opening the Rising Village shop, and in March 2016, we signed the lease for a 1,000 square foot space on Route 66 near downtown Tulsa. I said a sincere thanks and goodbye to Jerry and the baseball office, and we both promised to continue to spread the word about the other's nonprofit. He was starting a t-shirt business to help supplement donations, and we lamented about being the people our friends avoid.

"Maybe every nonprofit needs an income-producing business," he said after I moved the last of our products out of storage and returned the key. He was tinkering with his new embroidery machine, which had replaced our products and displays in the back lobby.

"I think so too. And besides, I'm tired of begging for donations," I said, and he looked up and smiled.

"You might be in the wrong business."

The board also approved hiring someone to help run the shop, and after interviewing several people, I found her. Jen had completed her graduate school practicum with Rising Village and traveled to Ghana with us the previous summer. She liked the idea of the shop, but her heart leaned toward the students, so I told her she would enjoy the benefit of a dual focus: liaison for sponsors in the U.S. and students in Ghana, and manager of a retail shop.

I wanted to be transparent with her. "I know this is a smaller salary than your previous job. Also, I don't know if the shop will work. It might only last a month or two. We're just going for it."

We were meeting at a coffee shop on a day when I was exhausted and running on two hours of sleep. I had been up most of the night, worrying I had jumped off the cliff of a crazy idea and was dragging people down with me. The cheerleader spirit of the board meeting had vanished, replaced with a low hum of apprehension.

"It sounds scary." Jen had been taking notes during our conversation with her rainbow-of-colors flair pens, and she closed her spiral notebook and packed the pens in a fabric case that would become familiar over the next two years. She looked at me and nodded. "I'm going to go for it, too."

Our intern from the previous summer, Maddy, was back with us and joined Jen, Kyle and me in transforming the space on Route 66. The building was newly renovated, and its exposed ductwork and brick walls gave it a rustic feel that reflected the handmade products we would sell.

We hung our "Rising Village Shop" sign outside above the door and met our next-door neighbor, Tasha, who had an extra cabinet we could use in our checkout area. We learned this area is called a cash wrap, and having a special type of cabinet is a must. Tasha happily loaned us the cash wrap cabinet and told us we should make it ours. "I don't need it back," she said. As we learned how to "retail," we found that most of the answers we needed were next door, where Tasha was more than happy to help. We pounded sheet metal and wood on the front of the cash wrap cabinet and hung giant colorful letters that spelled R-i-s-e, then tied strips of batik fabric to a room divider frame and set it behind the checkout stand. We gathered tables from flea markets and garage sales, and an antique dresser we found on the curb with a cardboard sign that said "freebie." Tasha also gave us a solid-wood headboard that we painted and placed on two tall stacks of cinderblocks to make a coffee bar. Our new home would be a store in the front half, with office and event space in the back half. The front was a wall of glass, which forced us to learn the art of window display and spotlighted the dust that accumulated each week. We painted the back wall gray and hung a silhouette map of the globe and pictures of the students in Ghana.

Kyle, whose time had come, was recruited for construction projects. He built rolling pallet walls, and we hung products, more photos of women and students, and a television on one pallet, so we could show videos of the families in Ghana. We slid a pallet wall halfway across a small area in the back for office space and brought in two wood tables that a church had loaned us. Our workspace was tiny, and Jen and I backed our chairs into each other most days.

On May 30, 2016, we turned over the chalkboard "Open" sign on our glass door and invited our community into the Rising Village Shop.

FACEBOOK POST, MAY 28, 2016

We've cleaned, built, stitched, tagged, decorated, priced, laughed, cried and come to the (almost) end of preparing the Rising Village space for opening. What a journey we're on! So here is a peek inside. We'll open our doors (it's just one door actually) at our new location on Wednesday, June 1. Come visit us on Route 66. We're excited to welcome you inside to shop, connect, and create!

CHAPTER SEVEN

Doing Business

BLOG POST DRAFT, AUGUST 31, 2016

I love a good spool table. They aren't really tables, but giant reels used to transport fiber optic cables and wire products. Because it's human nature to repurpose, someone transformed them, and presto—we now pay good money for these trendy little pieces of quasi-furniture. Which is why I snapped one up at the vintage market where I spent many hours hunting decor for the Rising Village Shop. It was a great price, so I paid for it and the shop owner and I loaded the table in the back of my car.

"One thing," she said before we started rolling it to my car. "It has a beer bottle inside, and the hole in the table is not quite large enough for the bottle to fall out. You'll have to figure some way to fish

the bottle out if you don't want it in there." As we rolled the table, I could hear the bottle rattling inside the hollow center. But it was a great price, and I didn't care.

When I drove up to the shop, Jen hurried out to help me unload my find. "It has a beer bottle in inside," I told her as we rolled the cable toward the door. "But I don't care. It can stay in there. It would be impossible to get it out." We had the spool table halfway inside the door when I realized we needed that beer bottle.

Removing it involved turning over the table, fashioning a hook from a coat hanger that could slide inside the bottle's neck, gingerly lifting it so that the hook didn't pop out, and keeping the bottle steady enough to fit through the opening. It was an activity more suited for a back alley than a retail sidewalk, and I was grateful our neighbors on either side weren't in yet.

Jen and I cheered and threw a high five when the bottle slid out—coat hanger still lodged in its neck. We rolled the table into our shop and adorned it with a display of braided fabric bracelets made by hairstylist apprentices in Ghana, Faustina and Joyce. We put a framed photo of the ladies near the bracelets. Our little table has great purpose. I took the beer bottle home, cleaned it up and purchased dainty silk flowers to draw attention to it on the table with the African bead jewelry. This discarded bottle has a story to tell: once trapped in a cable spool because whoever held the bottle last discarded it. The bottle was trash. Now, it holds silk flowers and is between two necklaces that are made with recycled glass beads. When we are explaining to our customers about the beads, we can point to our rescued vase and explain that the beads had once been discarded beer bottles, jars, windshields, glass containers. Trash. But someone gathered them up, and through crush-ing, mixing, molding, painting, and firing, the broken glass became a beautiful bead. I love the story our beer bottle tells because I want *that to be the story. Everyone matters—even those who we think are hopeless (that includes ourselves) and we all have the potential to be transformed. The world might look very different if we lived each day like we believe this is true. It's at least worth trying.*

Most people who came to Rising Village's store on Route 66 weren't thinking about changing the world, they just wanted to shop. And to be left alone in the process. But they had come to the wrong place if they wanted a solitary shopping experience, not only because Jen and I had a practiced sales pitch, but because our products had stories we intended to share.

"Have you been in before?" We began. During the first few months, we had mostly new customers, so the answer led us into a long explanation of who we were, what we sold, why it was special, and how purchases made a difference for families in Ghana. We pointed to photographs of the women and students, and even though you could see every square foot of our shop standing in one place, we gave visitors a tour anyway. We finished by asking if they had questions we could answer.

It took us six months to realize that almost no one wanted this, but we enthusiastically answered follow-up questions for the few who seemed to enjoy our tour. Most people wanted the freedom to browse, hold things in front of a mirror, text and chat on their cell phone, then wander out the door empty-handed. They cringed when we shouted, "You didn't find anything you couldn't live without?"

Minding the shop was much easier than figuring out the psychology of the shoppers. I am easily overwhelmed while shopping, so I try to avoid it. Multiple options confuse me and I'm nervous about spending money. About half of what I purchase goes back to the store after a shopping excursion, and if I keep things, my guilt level won't allow me to enjoy them for at least a week.

"You can shop guilt-free here," we told customers. "We're a nonprofit, so everything goes back into the organization."

"Then how do you pay your bills?" an irritated husband asked after we forced him to listen to the pitch while his wife wandered off. "I mean, your landlord and the utility companies aren't a nonprofit, right?"

He was right. Paying bills was not optional, but neither was paying the seamstress apprentices for the products we sold. At that point, the numbers were all working, and we could pay everyone, but his words sounded a tiny alarm that grew louder over the coming months.

A week later, I made a large wooden sign during an event at a local business. I chose a quote, burned it into the wood, and propped it against the main display table so customers couldn't miss it when they walked in the door.

Every time you shop, you're casting a vote for the kind of world you want.

I had read about "fast fashion" and the horrid working conditions in overseas factories where many of our budget-friendly clothes are made. Fast fashion is a manufacturing method focused on producing high volumes of clothing at a rapid pace. It utilizes trend replication and low-quality materials (like synthetic fabrics) to manufacture garments and bring inexpensive styles to the public. These cheaply made, trendy pieces result in overwhelming amounts of consumption. It also results in harmful impacts to the environment, garment workers, and, ultimately, consumers' wallets. The flip side of this is fair trade certified products that guarantee conditions in factories are environmentally friendly, safe for workers, and fair in wages. Jen and I started looking for companies that sold fair trade certified products we could add to our inventory. Adding products would bring in more profit and give shoppers more choices. We started with Global Mamas, a social enterprise that employed seamstresses in Ghana, then added other companies from Ghana, along with two from India and Tanzania. We purchased wholesale, tagged the products with the suggested retail price, and shifted displays around to make room for the fair-trade additions: chocolate bars, children's clothing, Bolga baskets from Ghana, leather bags from India, coffee from Tanzania. We also purchased and sold jewelry from a local woman who was a Native American member of the Creek Nation.

We also ordered one-yard pieces of wholesale batik fabric from Global Mamas in Ghana, designed and created by the women in their programs. Jen took the fabric and sewed pillows, stuffed animals, and decor on a donated Bernina sewing machine at the back of the shop. Customers loved the batik fabric, and one day Jen came up with an engaging way to share the women's stories. The idea combined her creativity with our customers' fascination with batik.

We had designated our three round tables at the back of the shop for donor gatherings, but most of the time, we used them to unpack the wholesale inventory. "What if we had parties to teach people how to batik?" Jen said as we were sorting the fabric for her sewing projects. I loved the idea, never mind that we didn't know how to batik. The method used in Ghana is stamping the wax on fabric with large wooden blocks, painting layers of color over the wax, and then boiling it in steaming cauldrons while stirring it with a stick. It's the method I had described to the men at Jerry's workout facility, but here, we could offer people the opportunity to create their own batik design. We decided to run videos of the Ghanaian process during our parties but found an easier method using tjanting brushes and beeswax.

Jen did hours of research and tested the method at her house. "It's kind of a pain," she said, "but we should do this anyway. We'll figure it out as we go along."

We charged twenty dollars per person, seated them at the round tables and taught them our method of batik. The path to the tables wound through displays of our products, and participants almost always made a purchase. We added birthday parties for children, stayed open late on nights when the art gallery down the street held an exhibition, did story time for young children, held our board meetings at the shop, and offered the back area and our three tables as a small event space. No one took us up on the event space idea, so we got desperate enough to host a shopping event with a multi-level marketing retailer. This was the opposite of fair trade, and when I pressed her on ethical standards of production, she assured me that their factories were "very fair." As she set up her racks of leggings and cotton dresses in the back area, I knew that acts of desperation like this meant our little shop was in danger of not making it.

"We'll do craft fairs and home parties again," I told Kyle one night when we were talking about ways to keep the shop open. "We can pack up products and take them on the road."

Recently, I ran across a memory on social media—a photo of suitcases and displays waiting to be loaded in my car. The post was cheery, and once again, we offered to bring the shop to homes or events. "Say the word and we're there!" But our dispositions weren't cheery and packing up the products to haul somewhere else and sell felt like a defeat.

We could still pay our seamstress apprentices, but after a year, the bills associated with the shop, our two small salaries, and funding the Ghana programs had caused a continued backward slide. The Christmas season in 2016 brought us out of our first slump, but by May of the following year, I knew we wouldn't make it to another holiday season. When I had presented the idea of a shop to the board, I told them there would be someone who would believe in it enough to donate funds for overhead costs. Our model was unique and progressive, and there were people who would love the shop enough to keep it open. That was probably true, but those donors hadn't walked through our door, and Jen and I were too busy trying to keep that door open to find them. On a hot July morning, fourteen months after our grand opening, Jen and I sat at a back table with our calendars and scheduled our final closing date.

If we hadn't been so exhausted, we might have been able to mourn properly. Jen was ready to move on to a full-time job where she could use her degree in Urban Youth Studies, and the day we said goodbye for the last time, the shop was almost empty. We had packed up the remaining inventory, returned the refurbished cash wrap, and sold most of the displays, including the rolling pallet walls Kyle had designed and constructed from scratch.

"It was an experience," Jen said, and I agreed. We learned valuable lessons, like how to create eye-catching window displays, reshape Bolga baskets that were flattened for shipping, and the importance of fresh flowers on the outside table. Also, we learned that my idea to burn incense on the inside of the shop smelled good, but it created a smoky haze (I eventually transitioned to candles). We knew how to troubleshoot technical issues with the point of sale and welcome the homeless people who wandered into our shop needing a cold drink.

Dealing with the issues in Ghana, however, was becoming more difficult. Regina and Abigail had completed their seamstress apprenticeships but over the three years, neither of them saved enough money to start their businesses. Throughout their apprenticeship, Isaac held quarterly workshops that stressed the importance of saving money for start-up costs, but there was no way to force it. Funding the start-up costs wasn't a precedent we wanted to set.

During our time in the shop, Isaac had expanded Rising Village further into the more under-resourced northern regions. We began providing micro-loans to basketweavers and batikers so they could expand their small businesses and added two staff in the region. But it was becoming difficult to maintain a structure and cohesive organization with programs spread across the country. Isaac held down a full-time job at the hospital, which meant most of his Rising Village work had to be done on evenings and weekends. It was getting complicated.

After the women in the north repaid the micro-loans, we decided to end our program in that region, and enter no more women into the apprenticeship program in the Ashanti region. It was a hard decision, but we were stretched too thin. We would walk beside the women who were still with us, but we wouldn't add more.

Back in 2014, I made a scrapbook album with a photo and story for each of our five students and four apprentices. I carried it to events and introduced people to the "Rising Village Family," adding to it every time a woman or student entered the program. Eventually the book was at its page capacity, so I put it in a box with the Colorado notebooks and other early nonprofit memorabilia. I found the box again after we moved the leftover shop inventory to the basement in our house, and I sat down on the cold concrete floor to flip through the pages.

Everyone in nonprofit work probably has that moment of wondering if it will ever be enough. Had we done enough to keep the shop open? Were we doing enough for the women and children? What did enough look like? I still felt a sense of injustice on behalf of vulnerable women and children in Ghana, but each page of that scrapbook held photos of people whose quality of life was a little better because they learned a skill or passed another grade in school. Like the scrapbook, our capacity was limited. Additional needs that surfaced often overwhelmed Ghana staff, and they found themselves "on call" after working hours. Adding more women and children would mean adding more staff, which meant more people for Isaac to manage, and more funds needed.

I wasn't in Ghana, and I didn't know how to fix it.

Sampson was the last student included in the scrapbook, and like the other children and apprentices, we committed to seeing him through the length of our program. It would be nine more years for Sampson. The first time we met him, he hid from us because we were white, but by the end of the day he was begging us to video him dancing, which we did. I looked at a photo of him with his elderly grandmother, Rose, who had her name tattooed on her arm as a young child, so if she was orphaned, her identity wouldn't be lost. As I turned the pages of the scrapbook and re-told myself stories of each child, mother and caregiver, Ghana felt far away and still unknowable. I put the Rising Village scrapbook into the box, along with a few items from the shop, and placed it at the front of a crowded shelf. There would be many more days when I needed a reminder that we had done good work, at least the best we could do. It was still hard to accept the small, incremental motion when what I longed for was big dramatic movements. Someday, I hoped it would feel like enough.

BLOG POST EXCERPT, SEPTEMBER 26, 2017

I want to believe that those of us who work cross-culturally care deeply about what we do and the people we work with, and yet it seems we spend so little time learning from them. We talk and talk, and then we board a plane and depart, knowing little more about the depths of the culture we have been in than when we arrived. So, I'm going to ease out on a limb slowly and carefully and say it: This is not an issue of how informed we are. It's an issue of how much we care about how informed we are.

Being informed can be risky. If we listen and learn, then discover our good works might actually bring harm or are not as effective as we had hoped and promised, then what do we do with that information? Some just continue to stumble down the road with their message and methods because, to be honest, we may not want to discover that our work benefits us far more than it benefits the people we seek to help. And what if, after all that listening, we're at a loss for an answer?

Here's my proposal: For a while, let's lay aside our brilliant ideas; tuck away our prepared spiel and glad tidings; tear up our agendas and rethink our missions. And then, let's be quiet and really listen, learn, and posture ourselves in humility and radical solidarity with all people in real places.

CHAPTER EIGHT

Welcome

BLOG POST APRIL 1, 2018

My proclamation a few weeks before Lent began—that I was giving up grumbling for six weeks—was probably a relief for the people who live in my house. While everyone else deprived themselves of chocolate and soda, I vowed to stop whining and groaning about every little winter thing that had been crawling under my skin for the past three months. Cold weather became my cranky catalyst, and it had gotten so bad that even I was tired of listening to myself.

Having settled the question of what would be given up, I was ready for Ash Wednesday. Then, the Sunday before Lent began, I ended up at a venue in Oklahoma City with a group of passionate advocates who had gathered to talk about the immigration and refugee crisis. I was tagging along with Kyle, who was interested in how he could dust off his law degree and put it to use on behalf of this population. I was happy to take a quick road trip with him on a Sunday afternoon. It would be fun. We'd drive and talk, and after it was over, find a quaint coffee shop.

For six years, I've had my head, heart, and sometimes my body in Ghana, working to help provide income sustainability and education to marginalized women and children in tiny rural villages spread across the West African country. The issue of immigrants entering and living in our country and the global refugee crisis is something I've only seen out of the corner of my eye. I paid closer attention to it during the presidential campaign as the rhetoric increased, culminating in the President's travel ban in February 2017. But still, I was too distracted to realize something was building.

In January 2017, Kyle and I downsized everything in our lives, including our house. For the previous year, we had been asking our own "what if" questions. At first, they seemed ridiculous and scary, and then they started to make some sense. After a while, they were the only thing that made sense. So, we sold our big house on one side of town, and moved into a much smaller, 90-year-old fixer upper on the other side of town. Our nonprofit work had left us with a dwindling nest egg, and after being in Ghana, so many things about our consumer-driven culture made less sense to me. We had been caught up in it for long enough, and although we had no illusions we would escape it completely, we wanted to curb the "more is better" mentality.

Our new neighborhood was filled with historic homes, most with large front porches, some refurbished and others on the verge of collapse, but we loved the diversity and openness of our new community. Our house sat on a slight hill, with a long climb of stairs to reach the front door, and three flights inside if we counted the basement. The floors slanted in certain rooms, and the windows were drafty in the winter. This was the first old home I had lived in, and the different styles in our neighborhood fascinated me. Every night, we took our dog, Grace, on walks to study the different houses and meet the neighbors. On one of our walks, a month before the shop closed, I stopped in front of the vacant church at the end of our street and stared at it. "That could be interesting."

"What are you thinking?" Kyle asked.

"We can't fit all the shop inventory and the displays in our basement," I said, which was true.

He shook his head. "We don't know what the inside of that place looks like, or if they are open to a nonprofit doing...what is it we would do there?" He pulled Grace up the hill, further away from the church on the corner.

"We could set up a place for pop-ups," I called up to him. He kept walking. "No more craft fairs," I called louder. It made sense, especially since I had continued to buy inventory from fair trade companies in India and Ghana, adding to the few products we had left from the apprentices. Jerry's words kept coming back to me, "Maybe every nonprofit should have a side business." Now that the shop was closing, I didn't want the side business returned to my house. That would feel like a backwards loop. At a board meeting, someone joked I should get a tattoo that said, "I love craft fairs." Except I didn't love them, and volunteers seemed to run from them. Three faithful volunteers were still hanging on, including Kyle, but he wouldn't last much longer. We still needed our nonprofit side hustle, and we needed space.

Three days later, I found the owner of that old church building and called her to ask if she would let a nonprofit use it for pop-up shops and storage. She agreed to let us lease the space for a year if we would cover the utilities. I eagerly signed a contract, and we moved the inventory and remaining displays out of the shop and into a rock church building with a sanctuary, offices, and an apartment upstairs. It was all in terrible shape except the sanctuary, which was cleared of its pews. Without Jen, I wasn't confident I could set up a shop that looked creative and appealing, so I studied photos of our Route 66 shop on my phone and did my best to replicate the old layout. We had kept a few of the table displays, including the spool table, so it was front and center, greeting shoppers as they walked through the sanctuary doors.

It was winter, and in Oklahoma that could mean mild or frigid. The weather was mild for the first month of January, but it turned cold in February, and I realized the heat in the old church wasn't working well. No one took off their coat during Our Valentine's Day pop-up shop, and the electric bill at the end of the month was more than five months of utility bills at the shop. The heating unit, I learned, was electric, inefficient, and expensive. Even one more month of cold weather would put our finances in danger, but we had signed a year-long lease. I had been churning about what to do for a few days when the owner called to apologize about the exorbitant bill. "And also," she said, and hesitated. "I feel terrible about this, but we've decided to sell the building. I'm afraid you can't stay."

"We understand," I said, trying to keep from sounding relieved, which I was. The old church never felt permanent, and it didn't seem like a sacred space, but the sanctuary's stained glass had a certain effect on me. Decades ago, when the building was still a church, someone whose world was falling apart probably walked in and prayed for the faith to believe it was all going to work out. Stained glass looks like all the messy parts of life, thrown together with the light still shining through. The old church had the ugliest stained glass I've ever seen—no real pattern, just big angular pieces of glass in red, green, blue and yellow, but it was enough to remind me I needed to keep a little faith that it would all work out.

That weekend, Kyle and I bundled up in warm clothes and held our last sale as brick-and-mortar retailers. It was our neighbors who came and purchased our quirky displays, including an antique school desk and the old spool table, minus the beer bottle.

I hauled the inventory back to the basement of our house, feeling like carefully stitched threads were unraveling. For several days, I sat at my office desk in the little room off our kitchen and mostly stared out the window. I didn't know where to go from here. In the "things will be okay" column, recurring donations were covering the work in Ghana and the apprentices had completed their training. In the "everything is awful" column, it was difficult for Isaac to stay in touch with the women after they finished the program, so we didn't have many success stories to share once they scattered.

We always get to choose which column we focus on. I tend to park my thoughts in the "everything is awful" column, but our little nonprofit had done some good, and in order to keep going, I needed to turn my attention toward those things. Thirteen women had a certificate from the government that would allow them to get a job in a salon, seamstress shop, or set up a business with the machine we funded in their start-up costs.

And six women in the north had expanded their businesses and paid back their loans. Staring out the window above my desk, I wished for a different outcome in Ghana. There were many more women who needed help to disentangle themselves from dead-end petty trading jobs or escape vulnerable situations. We are taught to measure success by size, numbers, and "bigger is better." Nineteen women didn't seem like enough, but it was the number we would keep, and with it, the assurance they had the skills they needed to earn income. The rest of their story was out of my reach, but I was keeping a little faith, telling myself it would be okay, and listening closely for what came next.

I was cleaning out files one morning when I found papers from a grant we had applied for two years earlier. This particular foundation rejected us because, while it appeared we did good work in Ghana, they were looking for organizations that were paying attention to local needs.

"Apply again next year if you can show us how you are working in your own backyard," they told us.

It felt wrong to force Rising Village into local work unless we found a need that fit our mission, so we waited. "Mission drift" in the nonprofit world is a real thing, and it can sneak up, especially when things get tough. Countless other good deed opportunities can overshadow the original mission of an organization, and before long, the organization is drifting in a dozen different directions. Our mission was explicitly laid out in our nonprofit formation documents.

Rising Village Foundation is a nonprofit organization that works to improve the lives of villagers in developing countries. The organization

will create partnerships between U.S. individuals, organizations, and
churches with the purpose of providing resources, encouragement,
volunteers, and advocacy for those trapped in poverty.

But organizations, like people, are constantly evolving, taking in new information, adjusting to change, and asking, "What's next?" I didn't want to leave anything behind, but I also knew that there was something on the horizon. I just couldn't see it yet.

I was preparing for an online selling event when a friend told me she had volunteered to teach English as a Second Language with a local Burmese church congregation in Tulsa. "If you're not buried in work, want to join me?"

It was strange to say yes, since I had mostly exempted myself from any type of volunteering once we started the nonprofit. Years earlier, I had tutored several students in English, and in my early twenties had taken an ESL course so Kyle and I could start a small language program in our church. I felt qualified to take on this new volunteer opportunity, but my confidence would waiver in the coming months.

I knew nothing about the Burmese community in Tulsa, so I asked the coordinator of the program to connect me with someone who could help me understand the culture before we started classes. She gave me the number of the pastor of the Burmese congregation and assured me she spoke good English. Her name was Lun, and when she answered, I addressed her as pastor. She laughed. "Oh, no. I'm not the pastor. I just help the pastor."

"Maybe you can help me, too," I said, and then invited her to lunch.

Lun had been in the U.S. for ten years and spoke excellent

English. We met at a local restaurant, and she ordered chili and a milkshake, then settled in to tell me everything she thought I needed to know about Burmese people. Although the country is now called Myanmar, the people refer to themselves as Burmese. They are resourceful, hardworking, religious, gracious and have lots of children, she informed me. We talked about her family back in Myanmar and the religious persecution that drove them from their country and into refugee camps in Malaysia. Since the Burmese community in Tulsa is large, they tend to be insular, and less prone to learn English within the first few years. Most are Zomi, a tribe in the Chin region of Myanmar.

"How many Zomi Burmese are in Tulsa?" I asked.

"There are so many of us," she answered with a smile. "When you know, tell me."

I later learned that the Zomi Burmese population in Tulsa is at least 10,000, the largest in the country.

"I've talked too much," she said, sliding her chili bowl to the side. "Tell me more about what you do."

Lun and I had been talking for two hours, so I gave her the short version.

"Rising Village has been working in Ghana for five years with at-risk students and single mothers. We find sponsors for the students because most of them live with grandparents who can't afford to pay school fees. And we resource the women so they can enter apprenticeships and expand their businesses."

"Women," she nodded. "So important."

"Our income generation program there has ended, but thirteen women finished apprenticeships in hairstyling and sewing."

Lun was reaching for her bag but set it down and put both palms on the table. She leaned forward.

"You taught sewing?"

"In Ghana," I said. "And it's the professional seamstresses who taught them, but we sourced funding so they could enter the program."

She leaned further toward me, nodding. "We can do this here. For the Burmese women."

"Do what here?" I asked.

"You can teach them to sew!"

She locked her eyes on mine, palms still flat on the table.

"We can do this. So many of our women are in their apartments all day with their children. They want to do something with their hands. They ask about this."

I sat back in the booth seat and contemplated the word "we." I knew Lun meant every word and was already five steps ahead of me. Some of the women had sewing machines, and others did not, but they could share in class. Maybe they could make children's clothing. There were so many possibilities. She was talking rapidly now, her eyes darting around as ideas came to her.

"Maybe some women want to make money by sewing so they can contribute to the family's income."

Sometimes, the neon sign is a dark-haired Burmese woman with fire in her eyes and a look of determination, and you're certain which direction to point your feet. I wanted to catch up to her. "I don't sew," I said, and she widened her eyes, as if this was good news.

"Me neither!"

I took it as another sign.

There were refugee sewing organizations scattered across the country, but not one in Tulsa. I began studying websites and Facebook pages and learned that sewing classes provide relationship benefits, English practice, and the opportunity for refugee women to learn skills that bring in extra income. But the overall benefit is integration. When the women are out in the community, meeting others, learning and using skills outside the home, they feel a sense of belonging. The sewing organizations I studied provided not only training classes, but a welcome for women from all over the world.

Lun told me that while many husbands of the Burmese women in Tulsa worked long shift hours at two local factories, the women were at home with children. Their language challenges kept them from moving freely through the community in ways we take for granted.

Lun was ready to get started, but first we needed to find instructors, so I asked a friend, Lenora, if I could come to her house and talk about sewing. She agreed, and we sat in her living room while I explained the concept to her.

"I'm not a professional seamstress," she said.

"Doesn't matter."

"I've never taught sewing."

"That's okay."

"I don't speak the language."

"You don't need to speak the language," I told her. "You just need to know how to sew. And care."

She looked up, thinking, and then back at me.

"I've never done anything like this."

"Me neither," I said. "Which is why we should do it."

Lenora was our first volunteer, and as we looked for a place to hold our sewing class, I continued to research similar programs. I studied the issues around the refugee and immigrant crisis in other countries, and the challenges refugees face in the U.S. I wasn't much of an ESL teacher, but I stumbled along on Sunday nights, and spent the rest of the week doing research.

I wanted to replicate Make Welcome, a program in Charlotte, North Carolina. They offered three levels of classes and partnered the refugee women with local businesses that did small-scale textile manufacturing. One afternoon, I was sitting on our back deck scrolling Make Welcome's Facebook page and ran across a post from their director, Beth, with an update on a former student. Ciin had completed three levels of the Make Welcome sewing program and had just moved to a new city. She was now teaching five women how to sew in her apartment on Friday afternoons.

We miss you, Ciin, the last sentence of Beth's post read, *but we're so glad you're helping women in Tulsa learn the skill of sewing.*

I reread the sentence and looked around my backyard. Ciin, a Burmese woman who had gone through the Make Welcome program, had moved away. And of all the cities she could have landed in, she was here in Tulsa. There was no way we weren't doing this. I quickly sent a direct message to Make Welcome's director and she responded the next day with an invitation to call her, which I did.

"I can't believe this," Beth said. "Ciin was one of our best students. She was worried she wouldn't find a sewing program in Tulsa."

I told her we hadn't started yet because we were looking for more instructors.

"She speaks good English, so you'll have a translator and an instructor," Beth said. "What's the name of your program?"

Once again, I had filled a notebook with ideas and had shared them with Lun. The name came easily.

"Our nonprofit is Rising Village, but the name of this program is Rise. Refugee Sewing Enterprise."

BLOG POST, APRIL 1, 2018

At the event in Oklahoma City, we heard from refugees, DACA recipients, advocates, immigrants, and those who were helping to resettle and serve people newly arrived in our country. They gave us facts and statistics, along with a few harsh realities. I got angry and sad. And then I realized how little I knew about an issue that was swirling in front of me, so I got motivated.

The Catholic activist Dorothy Day said, "our greatest danger is not our sins, but our indifference," to which I humbly offer the possibility that our indifference is the sin. This Lenten season I discovered that moving from indifference to informed can be a spiritual experience, and for me it is the prerequisite for any calling that involves doing the work of justice. So is prayer, lament, and meditating, which became more necessary as I read the stories of what people are enduring in conflict areas and refugee camps, and what they are facing daily in our own communities.

My work in Ghana continues as Rising Village provides resources so people can rise up and out of the margins. But I am also paying attention to what is happening in front of us—in our own community. My Lenten deep dive has moved me to join the courageous voices here, and then, in the spirit of my favorite African proverb, look for ways to "move my feet."

CHAPTER NINE

RiSE in Tulsa

BLOG POST, JUNE 12, 2018

Every Monday, we gather in the morning and afternoon with two groups of women who are both newly arrived in the U.S. and some who have been here for many years. There are 14 sewing machines on tables across a large room in a generous church in the south part of the city. We are just beginning, but already we see joy in the faces of the women—both students and volunteers. This program gives refugee women a way to contribute to their families as they learn how to mend and sew clothes—and for some women, earn income by stitching products they can sell. Our eight sewing instructors move around the room, helping the women learn the machine, the stitching, troubleshooting, and giving encouraging feedback. Amid the humming of machines, we are building relationships with one another through the act of creating.

In a world that seems increasingly divided and unwelcoming to those who need refuge, friendship and kindness, we believe that what goes on in that second-floor room in South Tulsa might be a small way to bring us back together and remind us we are all neighbors.

The day President Donald Trump signed the executive order blocking citizens of six predominantly Muslim countries from entering the U.S., Lun and I were searching for a location to hold our refugee sewing classes. I turned on the news in my car after the two of us had sat in a large room with party lights strung across the ceiling and ample space for her two children to play chase. The news reporter called it the most significant hardening of immigration policy in generations. Although Myanmar, was not on the list, refugees and immigrants, along with their advocates, were panicky.

Isaac had tried twice to get a visa to the U.S. and been denied, which was the closest I had been to any personal stake in our country's immigration policy. Now, with 21 women signed up for our first sewing skills training class, I paid closer attention to what was happening in our country. There seemed to be a palpable divide between those who thought we should fear an influx of people from other countries, and those who held out their arms to welcome them. In Ghana, we wanted the mothers and students to know they were an important part of their village, even if the messages society communicated to them were very different. In Tulsa, we wanted to bring voices of welcome, and send a louder message than those who shouted for immigrant bans and other fearful actions.

We visited Ciin in her small, two-bedroom apartment in the south part of Tulsa, where most of the Burmese refugees lived. When Beth, the director at Make Welcome, had texted Ciin to ask her if she would be interested in teaching sewing to a large group of women, she didn't hesitate. I called her on a Monday afternoon, and I could barely hear her over the child crying in the background.

"I would like to talk," she said in her soft voice. "Please come visit."

Lun directed me to take my shoes off and slide them next to the other pairs lined up on the small square porch. Ciin's sewing machine was on the kitchen table, with a stack of fabric beside it. The room was sparse, with three family photos on a wall, a calendar, and three folding chairs across from a couch. Five women who lived in the complex, also refugees, would come to her apartment tomorrow for their weekly sewing lesson. My mother had sewed alone, spreading her patterns out on the dining room table, ironing the fabric on a board set up by the sliding glass door, and requiring silence and solitude, so she could concentrate. She didn't invite friends over to sew in groups, although I had always heard my grandmother talk about sewing circles. This was what I imagined when Ciin talked about her five friends and the weekly lessons—a social opportunity that was as necessary as patterns, stitches, and finished products. It was this way in Ghana. Every seamstress shop was alive with gossip, laughter, advice, disagreements and, sometimes, singing. The women could rotate the crank with one hand, push the fabric through with the other, and tell a story from start to finish.

I could see why Lun was adamant that the Burmese women needed this kind of social interaction. Maybe my mother was content to sew alone, but the energy of creating while socializing appealed to me.

Ciin's young son sat in her lap, his head against her chest with one eye on me while we told his mother about the sewing classes. She nodded as we talked about our need for a translator who understood the culture and could help us design classes for non-English speakers. We already had twenty women signed up, we told her, and a waiting list of twenty more that was growing every day. She frowned and slid her young son from her lap.

I waited while she spoke in Burmese to Lun, worried the number of students was intimidating to her. We were trying to limit the number to ten per class, but that was still twice the number of women she was teaching in her apartment.

Lun turned to me, and before she could say anything I reminded her there would be other volunteers in the room, and Ciin wouldn't be alone.

"That isn't the problem," Lun said. "She wants to include her five Friday afternoon students in our classes."

That would be 26 students for our first beginner class. I could have hesitated, but everything up to this point had been like a neon sign that read: This is the way forward. If we wanted our welcoming voices to drown out the chorus of fear, we would always need to make room for a wider circle.

Our first class included 25 Burmese and one Venezuelan, Veronica. She was my assigned student in the ESL class and an asylum seeker who had fled the country with her husband and two daughters. She came to the U.S. speaking almost no English, and as her ESL tutor, I did little to help her with the language. The church that coordinated the class conducted our training in one evening, and our volunteer program met only once a week. Most English learners need daily classes, and volunteers like me need weeks of training. I wasn't sure our class was the best choice for people who were serious about learning English, but Veronica worked during the day and had no other option. Despite my shortcomings as a tutor, she was determined, and studied the language on her own throughout the week. Veronica would come to class on Sunday night more English literate than the week before, and graciously attribute her progress to my instruction, but I knew better. In Venezuela, she had been a college professor with a side hustle selling handmade stitched items at craft fairs and festivals. When she pulled up photos of denim headbands, bows, purses, and vests, I asked her if she wanted to join the first sewing class of our new program, RiSE.

"No machine," she said.

"After ten weeks of class, you'll have one," I told her.

Our language barrier kept me from explaining that for each class session attended, a student earned $7.50, and at the end of the semester, she would have $75 in credit to put toward a machine. We would purchase wholesale machines for $100, so students would only have to pay the rest, $25. It was enough that I promised her a sewing machine in ten weeks, and she signed up.

We found volunteers through local churches who wanted to help instruct and discovered that people who sew also hoard fabric they may never use, so donations piled up. The church where we held the classes funded our class machines and sewing supplies. It was a swirling mass of activity to prepare for the class and the entire program. The week before we started, I was in the room organizing fabric when a lady popped her head in the door.

"Is this the location of the sewing classes?"

She had a Spanish accent, and I invited her to see the room. "We'd love to have you join us, but we are full for this semester."

She told me her name was Elena, and then she shook her head and adjusted her glasses.

"I'm not here to sign up for the class. I was wondering if you needed more volunteers."

I told Elena about Veronica and she put her hands together and looked up.

"Then God brought me here for a reason. I'm here for Veronica."

It went like that for the four weeks we were preparing for classes. Details fell into place and needs were met, but I still did my share of overthinking, determined to make that first day perfect. Each instructor received an overly detailed notebook, and I placed three sheets of paper beside each machine that explained our program in simple English, along with a binder for keeping patterns and more papers. I arrived early on the first day, along with an instructor named Dede who volunteered to help me set up the twelve machines we had purchased for class training. My hands were sweating.

Everything was up close now that we were working in our "backyard." I felt responsible for making sure volunteers and students had an enjoyable experience, and that donors saw our program as successful. It wasn't something we only did over there, in a faraway location where most people would never visit. It was happening here.

"You seem nervous," Dede said as we plugged the machines into extension cords that snaked between the tables.

I explained how strange it felt to be this close to one of our programs. "It's like the nonprofit just jumped in front of my face."

She stood up and looked around the room.

"I think it's going to be fun," she pointed to the ceiling. "Remember, we have party lights. Let's plug them in."

My phone vibrated with a text as I plugged in the lights. It was from one of our board members and the pastor of the church where we held classes.

You okay if Channel 8 comes to do a news story about RiSE this morning?

Lun was just walking in the door, and I showed her the text.

"Is it going to bother the women if they're on the news?" I asked.

Her mouth opened in surprise.

"They will love it!"

I thought about how often refugees are invisible in their communities, contributing quietly, paying their taxes, and taking care of their families. I answered the text. *We're more than okay with it.* Today, these women in our village would be visible.

The story of RiSE started in a church Sunday school room, but we quickly moved to a room in CarePoint, a refugee resource center in the heart of the Burmese community in Tulsa. In the new location, we had expanded storage space for the donations of fabric, supplies, extra machines, and everything that kept piling up as classes continued. The hum of activity at CarePoint included ESL classes, health classes for women, a clothing room and special events like a prom dress shopping night and a Christmas room. There was always something happening, and our sewing classes fit in with the services already provided. Sometimes, it was hard for people to distinguish the RiSE program as part of a separate nonprofit, so I put a Rising Village sign out by the entrance door for sewing classes, the one that hung above our shop door on Route 66. I also corrected people when they referred to RiSE as part of CarePoint. "We are actually a 501(c)(3), formed in 2013. We also work in Ghana," I would tell them.

During our second year of the RiSE program, we purchased fabric made by the women in our micro-loan program in Bunk-rugu, Ghana, Comfort and Hannah. They had paid back their loans and together opened a small shop where they sold the colorful fabric designed using blocks of *Adinkra* symbols. Isaac shipped over four yards of green, blue and purple fabric with swirls, dots, squares and circles and we included the fabric in the stack of choices for our skirt-making class.

By the time we moved into our sewing room at CarePoint, refugee and immigrant women from all over the world were participating in our classes. We taught women from Peru, Iran, China, Taiwan, Russia, Jordan, Lebanon, Chile, and a new student from the Congo, a tall eighteen-year-old, named Aline. She and her family had come to the U.S. six months earlier, and their resettlement caseworker had told us they were having a hard time adjusting. There were few Congolese in Tulsa, and the mother and oldest daughter needed a circle of friends.

Aline smiled shyly when she spotted the fabric from Ghana in the pile, and she pulled out a yard of the purple design.

"This looks like Africa," she said in an almost-whisper as she unfolded the fabric and held it up to her waist. The pattern was a wrap-skirt, similar to what the women wore in her country. It felt like a full circle, or at least a winding road that led from Ghana to Tulsa, keeping the two programs connected.

By the end of the second year of RiSE classes, we had a waiting list of almost 40 women. We held three beginner classes with 30 students, two advanced classes with ten students each, and a workshop for those who wanted to earn income by stitching products we sold on the website. Since it was important to toss around numbers, I let people know that 131 women had passed through our program during those two years.

Despite the impressive number of RiSE program participants, few were earning income. We were in our third year, and less than ten women had either found employment in textile shops or jobs sewing from home. Ciin was one woman who could manage her family, the language challenges, and working with clients, but only if we connected her with them. We were working to find volunteers who could help with those connections.

"We need to do craft fairs," one of our instructors said soon after we had moved to CarePoint and started the workshop. I groaned, but I knew she was right. If we wanted to help the women earn income, we needed to peddle the products around to different venues. That craft fair tattoo was making more sense.

Everything seemed to pick up speed: classes, selling products, connecting the most advanced women with employers, planning workshops to help the income-earning women understand taxes and small business practices, and managing volunteers. When we worked in Ghana, being the only employee made sense, but this seemed out of control. I needed more full-time hands and feet. I felt that familiar slide into a frantic pace, and even though volunteers were more plentiful, we faced more needs that were outgrowths of sewing classes. We helped women enroll children in school, secure furniture for new relatives who were coming to the U.S., find part-time jobs for teenagers of the women in our program. In the middle of the chaos, we threw a Christmas party for the advanced students, and Lenora put together a "dirty Santa" gift exchange, which I thought would never work. We had to explain the concept a few times, and then assure the students that for the next hour, stealing was perfectly acceptable. The game was a joyous new discovery for the women, and in every photo of smiling, laughing faces, I see the connection we hoped for when we started the RiSE program. Every time I look back at those party photos, I experience a mixture of joy and sorrow. We had no idea what was coming.

A few days before Christmas, 2019, one of our volunteers sent me a message. *I think Martha's house was on the news.*

Martha was one of our advanced students, and Jill had given her a ride home after a few classes, so she recognized her house in a news story that aired one evening. It was the scene of a suicide and double murder. A father and two children.

"I'm sure it's not Martha's family," I texted. "All those houses look alike." It was unthinkable, so I put it out of my mind until the next day when Jill replied.

It's Martha's house.

Over the next week, we did our best to walk beside our friend through the horror of what had happened to her family. We cried along with her as we walked into the viewing room where the two boys were in a casket together and the father in one next to them. Lenora and I couldn't understand most of what family members were saying, but even when we speak the same language, there are no words for a tragedy that intense. We spoke with tears and hugs.

At the funeral the next day, someone handed me Martha's

two-year-old daughter, and I held her for the length of the service. She was coming down with a cold and was fussy, so I stroked her head and prayed there would be support for this family. The people who bring food, attend the service, send flowers and sympathy cards will usually move on a few weeks after a funeral and leave the family to navigate grief on their own. Maybe it was different in the Burmese community. Maybe the people would stay beside Martha through the long months and years of loss. Most of the two-hour service was in Burmese, but we could hear the pain, and we tried to feel hope sprinkled in.

Ghana had shown me how resilient we humans are. Even in dark, incomprehensible places of despair, people survive. But it takes a village.

"It's going to be okay," I whispered to Martha's daughter, Angela, as she fidgeted and whimpered throughout the funeral service. This was what it looked like to work in close proximity to the people you're serving. We weren't getting on a plane the next day to leave them. We were here.

I felt more determined after that, and we enrolled another group of 30 new students in mid-January and started classes in February. I had given in to another round of craft fairs, knowing it was the best way to sell what the women made. We assembled a team of volunteers and planned to travel to fairs at least once a month, so I got myself mentally prepared.

In my journal, on March 6, I didn't mention a virus that was traveling from China, Europe and was already in the U.S. It seemed impossible it would penetrate our borders and change our lives. My entry focused on a writing project and where Colin would move when his lease was up.

Then, on March 15, I wrote three pages about a virus that

forced us to shutter inside our homes, not shake hands or hug, wear a mask, and self-quarantine. We told the women it wasn't safe to be together anymore, and we canceled classes. "Please stay home and take care of yourselves and your families," I wrote to them in our online Viber group. "And I'm sure we'll be back together very soon."

FACEBOOK POST, MARCH 16, 2020

We are sad to announce that we are suspending ALL RiSE Sewing Classes until further notice. We want the very best outcome for our community, our students and their families, and although we will miss our weekly social integration, now is the time for social distance. It's important that we do our part to help mitigate the spread of COVID-19. We have several vulnerable families in our program who may have a difficult time navigating through these weeks (months), so we will mobilize helping hands who can meet needs of these families. In the meantime, we pray for peace, health, and safety as we journey through this time.

CHAPTER 10

Endings

JOURNAL ENTRY, MARCH 25, 2020

Sunday. We're all socked in and hiding from the coronavirus. We are told to practice social distancing and, as much as possible, "self-quarantine." At first, that made me edgy since I'm not an introvert and don't do well if I'm stuck in the house for long stretches. But as more news comes out about the virus's travel and effects, the more I'm feeling secure in the house and away from people. It's strange how quickly you can become wary of the person standing next to you—not knowing if they might expose you to the virus. We're told not to hug or shake hands. What was a very expected greeting only a week ago is now potentially dangerous, so we bump elbows or just wave, as if we are all too far away to attempt touching. And we are. Now that we're a danger to one another, we do relationships from a distance.

The streets were almost empty the Tuesday I drove to Care-Point. It was March 17, and over the past three days, everything in Tulsa had begun to slowly shut down. The pandemic had already hit hard in other states, but Oklahoma is in the middle of the country and geography puts us behind trends and curves. Now it was our turn. The previous Friday, the mayor asked that bars and restaurants close, and no one gather in groups of over 50. By the next Tuesday, they had reduced the group size to ten. CarePoint was empty except for the director, Kara, who was in her office on the computer.

I was there to pick up a large trash bag filled with care packages for our students and their families. After we canceled classes, volunteers assembled crayons, coloring pages, play dough, a sewing kit, and children's books we would deliver to the porches of 30 women. Diapers were in short supply because of hoarding, and some of our families were in need. Many of the women felt confused and afraid to leave their homes, so we offered to venture out and shop for them. Two volunteers were out scouring stores in between delivering their care packages the day I drove to CarePoint. After a week of puttering around the house, scrolling social media, and waving at neighbors from a safe distance, I needed to get out of my house and neighborhood for the day. The deliveries seemed like a safe way to stay busy.

As I was putting the trash bag in my truck, my phone delivered a message from the Rising Village website. A nurse from a local hospital was asking if we could make masks for the healthcare workers. The supply chain for everything seemed ground to a halt: toilet paper, hand sanitizer, bacterial wipes, rubbing alcohol. And face masks. The day before, Lenora was picking up sewing supplies at a local craft store and overheard a doctor's panicked request for help with face masks. He wanted to make them for the workers at his clinic, since they were running out of paper masks. He asked the employee if he could just use staples, interfacing and elastic. Lenora texted me with the story and asked whether we should think about having our women make masks.

"Let's get the care packages delivered," I told her. "Then we'll think about it."

After the message from the nurse, there were two more requests for masks before the end of the day. One message had a pattern attached. *Something like this?*

Everything was shutting down, but hospitals were slammed with patients and lacking supplies. The hospital-grade face masks were being reserved for doctors and nurses, and there were no facemasks available for support staff. They risked exposure without protective face coverings. The RiSE students could sew, and most were sitting in their homes with nothing to do. We had a storage wall of fabric, bins of elastic, and one of our instructors, Sydney, had been a pediatric nurse. She could alter the pattern that was sent to us and make it appropriate for support staff at hospitals and clinics. The three of us hurried back to CarePoint to gather supplies and contact some of our advanced students who could take Sydney's pattern and quickly sew masks. Language challenges meant that making a pattern was not enough. We would need to video the entire process so they didn't have to translate written instructions.

On Friday, with her eight-month-old son strapped to her back, Sydney set her phone on a tripod, and we helped her record a face mask sewing tutorial. We were in the middle of it when a local news station called to ask if they could do a story, and we agreed. It was a frenzy, but nothing we had done over the past seven years felt timelier and more necessary. The requests kept coming, and the refugee women were contributing to their community in a way none of us could have imagined.

In front of the news camera, Lenora talked about the doctor trying to make masks for his clinic, and Sydney clarified that the masks were for healthcare workers who were not on the front lines. She talked while assembling squares of fabric, elastic, and instructions for the seamstress's kits.

"The women in our program are ready to do this, and eager to give back to the community," I said. "We're going to get out as many as we can." I stood in front of the camera, hoping we could make at least 100 face masks, which seemed like an unrealistic goal. It would involve dropping off supplies on the seamstresses' doorsteps, picking up the finished masks, and delivering them to hospitals and clinics. Many of our volunteers were older and staying home, so only a few of us were still venturing out. Even though the pick-up and deliveries were safe, we didn't ask our volunteers to do anything that would make them uncomfortable during this strange time.

I was confident the three of us could handle the logistics. When I look back at the news video and read my journals from those first few weeks of the pandemic, it's clear we were unprepared for what was ahead.

We delivered facemask kits to 14 women, and in three days we had 41 masks, then 50, and by the end of two weeks, the women had made over 100 masks. We were getting requests from clinics, hospitals and nursing homes in Tulsa and neighboring towns. People were scared for relatives who worked in healthcare, and some of them called us, pleading for masks, and offering to come pick them up in five minutes. By the end of March, Oklahoma had the fourth highest death rate in the country, and the remaining volunteers who were still picking up and delivering supplies and finished masks worried about being out of their homes. Everyone was confused about how the virus was transmitted, and sometimes it felt like even the air we breathed might not be safe. Our volunteers hadn't signed up for this kind of operation, and they wondered how long we could sustain it. It was a reasonable concern, but the need for facemasks kept growing, morphing from healthcare workers to individuals, then companies who wanted to provide them for their employees. The women continued to sew, and Lenora, Sydney and I continued to drop off kits, pick up masks, then wash, dry and iron them. When the washing machine in our basement quit, I hurried over to one of our empty rental houses and washed masks all evening.

Many of the women in the RiSE program were struggling financially now that businesses were shutting down and laying off workers. The women who sewed masks for hospital workers had done a service for our community, but demand from the public was high, with no end in sight. It was time for the women to earn some income. As I thought back to what had moved me in Ghana, it was providing women avenues for income so they could stand up and feel proud they had supported their families. I remembered Regina, the first Rising Village seamstress apprentice, holding her sewing machine high above her head on our first trip to Ghana and declaring that every day, her daughter would see her working. Our mission was to help women become trained in a skill, then use that skill to put food on the table. We didn't believe that handouts for the long-term brought dignity or helped women rise.

Somewhere in Ghana, Regina, Abigail, and the other women who had finished their apprenticeships were sewing. I thought about them when I picked up masks in Tulsa and waved at the seamstresses through their screen doors or windows. As I traveled from house to house, I felt that same sense of pride for the women. I cheered on our refugee seamstresses in our Viber group chat.

You keep sewing the masks and we'll keep picking them up and delivering them wherever they are needed. We would continue until there was no more demand.

In addition to the deliveries we were making, I uploaded 65 masks to our online store, and we sold out in less than an hour. "No more washing, drying and ironing," I told Lenora. "We need to get them out the door fast."

Numbers were running through my head all day as I calculated how many masks each woman made and their earnings. I updated the spreadsheet on my phone every time I picked up and delivered. The bulk orders for companies were wrapped and waiting on my porch or at CarePoint when an employee hurried over for pick up. I wrote in my journal that it all felt like an adrenaline rush, and that my brain only shut down while I was sleeping. *One day, I think I'm going to hit a wall. And I'm sure I'm not alone.*

By April 14, the women had made over 1,500 masks. We used soft cotton fabric and tried to find unique designs that would lessen the drudgery of strapping on a mask for every outing. We took special requests for fabric with cats, dogs, flowers, camo, stars and stripes (4th of July) and unicorns. Most of the time, we found fabric for the custom orders in our donated stash. The bulk orders kept coming, and the online store kept selling out. Days went by in a blur of the same rotation: pick up masks, deliver supplies, ship, account for sales and income, communicate with Lenora, Sydney, and the seamstresses. The running felt like it was keeping me from losing my mind, but everyone in our family was getting edgy and snappy. Kyle and I argued about things that made no sense—pandemic spats, we called them.

The frantic pace seemed like wonderful therapy, and in addition to helping the women's financial situations, selling masks was helping to keep Rising Village out of financial danger. In April, we applied for the government's emergency pandemic "PPP" loan and received $1,000, which helped, but we depended on ongoing donors and sales. So far, the mask operation had inspired donors, and sales put us in a better financial position than we had been in two years. But everything felt unpredictable. I was sure that once supply chains for masks became re-established, the need would wane. It was May, and suddenly I had no idea what our future looked like. Some seamstresses who were no longer in a financial crisis wanted a break from sewing. By June, only five women were making face masks, and everyone was exhausted.

The last bulk order came in July, but the pandemic wasn't going away. Our state, and the entire country, couldn't seem to flatten the curve, and the threat of virus surges made everyone feel helpless. We had no choice but to postpone classes indefinitely. We couldn't teach sewing from a distance and our room wasn't large enough to stay six feet apart.

In September, it was clear our beginner students would not finish in person, so we graduated the women. They picked up their supplies for the last two projects, and I printed graduation certificates. We purchased their sewing machines and called it even on the credits. Their drive-through graduation was nothing compared with the six previous ceremonies, which had been more like parties with photos, food, hugs, and lots of laughter. This time, we wore masks and handed out congratulations and certificates at arm's length. Everyone seemed to be afraid of everyone else, even the people we had embraced without a thought two months earlier.

"Everything has a way of working out," Kyle reminded me, and this had been true for Rising Village since its beginning. We never had a five-year plan, certainly not an eight-year plan. Yet in the fall of 2020, our finances were healthy, and over 130 women had completed or were current students in the RiSE program. We needed to hang on until the pandemic passed so we could continue our work, face to face instead of distanced.

In 2014, during Rising Village's first year, I had just returned from Ghana and was sitting outside with Kyle and a glass of wine. The work was still fresh, donors were plentiful, and I felt energized. Isaac believed we could expand the work in ways we hadn't even thought of yet, and I was on board with exploring other areas of Ghana. We had big dreams.

I had been talking nonstop while Kyle listened, and after a while, we were both silent.

"There's a lot to look forward to," he said and stood up to get ready for bed. Something had been playing at the edges of my mind, and I voiced it.

"Rising Village doesn't belong to me." I felt it deeply, and it was a strange relief. "Someday I'll need to hand it over, and I hope I still feel this way."

He nodded. "Keep that thought and you will."

The thing about founding a nonprofit is you can confuse starting something with owning it. We had by-laws that clearly spelled out that our 501(c)3 corporation didn't belong to me, or anyone else. But I had poured myself into its formation and carried Rising Village with me everywhere I went. My conversations centered on it, my thoughts swirled around it, and every day I spent too many hours believing it was all up to me to keep it going. It felt very much like mine, and there were days my fingers clutched it too tightly.

After that evening, I would frequently remind myself that no matter how much Rising Village intertwined with my life, it was not mine to keep.

The pandemic forced us to halt everything, and after the mask production puttered to a stop, I had plenty of time to think. We were all changing; questioning, rethinking, shifting direction, and leaving things behind. I wrote pages in my journal about what it feels like when the world stops, and then I realized what had been my world for the past eight years was moving toward an end. It took a pandemic for me to remember that even though I loved this nonprofit, it wasn't mine, and the months of quarantine gave me the space and time to know someone else could love it just as much. I can't explain this. Sometimes we just need to stop moving long enough to know what's been circling around in our heart. *It's time to move on*, I wrote on June 3, 2020. Once the words were on paper, they made so much sense. Enough people had filled the coffee can, and I could hand it over knowing I held it long enough.

One of our board members, the pastor who first opened his church's doors to our new sewing program in Tulsa, had been thinking about starting a nonprofit focused on refugee services. "We have one," I told him. We hired our intern from five years earlier, Kelsey, to take over the RiSE program. She had traveled to Ghana with us in the early days and in my introduction on social media, I posted a photo of her at the sewing shop in Ankaase with Georgine, who was teaching her to use the hand-crank machine.

I handed Rising Village over to people who believed deeply in the mission and were equipped and ready to take it. I remain as founder, but it's just a title. Rising Village belongs to every person who has donated funds, served on the board, volunteered their time, and voiced a prayer on behalf of the women, students, and refugees.

There is no final report I could send with big numbers and amazing success stories, and I never learned to sew. If I was sitting in the red dirt circle, I would conclude my part in the Rising Village story by describing the old analog meters used in audio recordings. Those meters often couldn't pick up the low sounds that make the needle move, but when the meter picked up a faint sound, that needle jerked up a little. A small movement, and that's what comforts me. We moved the needle. The sound registered, and it changed lives, including mine. Starting and running a nonprofit humbled me, and probably aged me, but I don't know what else I could have done for those eight years that would have taught me more about myself, and the world. It was wonderfully exhausting, and now is in the hands of others who will move it forward in ways I never could.

Red dirt is caked on a pair of shoes I keep tucked far under my bed. I only wore them in Ghana, and I can't bear to clean the dirt out of the bottom grooves. If I had been more intentional, I would have taken a handful of gritty Ankaase dirt and kept it in a jar to remind me of a place that holds my heart. Then I would have mixed it with brown dirt from this eastern part of Oklahoma, where Afghan refugees have started arriving and need welcoming. I'm going to keep moving my feet, taking another step, then another, maybe moving the needle a bit as I go. People do this every day—take one small scary step and go from there. It's what changes the world and gives us a story to share when we're asked for news from the road.

BLOG POST, AUGUST 20, 2020

I'm thinking about risk these days, and how it stretches our faith, causes our hearts to pound, and makes the craziest ideas seem absolutely beautiful.

EPILOGUE

On a breezy Tuesday night in February 2022, I arrived at
CarePoint to drive five Afghan women home from sewing class.
Since my transition from executive director, I now considered
myself a volunteer, and was eager to help whenever possible.
The women were part of a large group of Afghan refugees who
escaped the country beginning in August 2021 after a revitalized
Taliban took control of Kabul. Many Afghans fled, including the
nineteen women who attended RiSE sewing class on Monday
evenings. As the women walked to my car, I could see they were
carrying bags they had made in class that evening and I recognized the pattern. The Ankaase Bag. This was the first project
our apprentices in Ghana learned to sew for income—and had
always been final project in our RiSE Sewing Basics classes. As
I watched the women climb into my car, the bags either folded
in their arms or slung across their shoulder, I wanted to explain
everything about that bag—the first women who had made it,
how we filled suitcases with the bags to bring back from Ghana,

my college roommate who designed the bag. We had a language barrier, so I sat for a minute and thought about how to explain this beautiful full circle.

"These bags," I said, pointing at one, and the women looked at me expectantly. But the story was too long, and our languages were too different. So, I simply said, "I love them."

They held up their bags and nodded in agreement, smiling at me. Those bags aren't going to change the world, but for a group of women in the Monday night Sewing Basics class, they represent a welcoming open door, and a desire by one group of people to hold out their hands to another group of people. We'll keep doing this, and together we'll make small movements of change that just might leave the world a little better than we found it.

To learn more about Rising Village Foundation, visit risingvillage.org.

The proceeds from this book benefit Rising Village Foundation.

ACKNOWLEDGEMENTS

I almost didn't include this because the list is too long, but it seems wrong to not give thanks. So many people believed in this little nonprofit we call Rising Village, and without them we couldn't have survived.

Peter and Anna were gracious teachers and honest partners. Thank you for the invitation to Ghana.

Much like my family, Isaac's pulled together to help Rising Village fulfill its mission on those red dirt roads. Thank you to Victor, who continues to teach, mentor, and counsel the students in our sponsorship program. And I am grateful to Dr. and Mrs. Akromah for the ways they have opened their home and hearts to the Rising Village women and students.

Nonprofits don't exist without supporters, donors, and volunteers. On days when it felt futile, I would recall the people who gave energy and resources to Rising Village and expected nothing in return. They always gave me the hope to keep going.

The strong women who successfully completed our program,

started, or expanded their business and provided for their families deserve more than a simple acknowledgment at the end of a book. They showed me gritty resilience and a commitment to their children that still humbles me.

The Lobeck Taylor Family Foundation in Tulsa stepped out and took a risk on our new RiSE program. The grant they funded allowed us to move forward with our dream of providing equipment and income-producing opportunities for refugee women.

As the RiSE program expanded, our friends at CarePoint, and its director, Kara Lee, were gracious to allow us more room for storage, and anything we needed in their resource center to successfully grow our sewing program.

Our board of directors has been my sounding board, therapy group, dinner companions, travel buddies, voices of reason, and faithful friends. I could not have asked for a better group to guide and lead this organization.

Meeting Isaac Akromah was not a random moment. My life would be so different if he hadn't walked into the Methodist Church in Ankaase. Our lives will continue to move in different directions, but I will never forget belting out country music together on a backroad in Ghana, the many meals we've shared, the problems we've solved (and left unsolved) and the places we've traveled together. Isaac has walked, driven, and flown many miles to move the needle.

My partners at Storia Publishing, Megan, Katy, and Juli were patient and encouraging, and tough when necessary. I'm indebted to their help in birthing this book.

Thank you Maddy, Kelsey, Jen, Lenora, Sydney, and Chris for pouring yourselves into the work.

Colin, Erin, and Alison Tresch have done more than any three offspring should have been asked to do for this nonprofit. Thank you for what you have done, and that you never complained about doing it.

And to Kyle, who has been the definition of my other half, not just over the past eight years, but for the past 32. Thank you for treating Rising Village so well, and for giving me the push and pull to move forward and step back exactly when I needed to. Your honesty and commitment to the cause has kept me on the road.

ABOUT THE AUTHOR

 Lisa Jackson Tresch has a B.A. in Journalism, worked as a reporter for the *Tulsa World* newspaper and was editor of *Mia*, a magazine featuring the voices and stories of women. She has ghostwritten three books and worked as a freelance editor before launching the nonprofit, Rising Village Foundation. This is her second memoir. She lives in Tulsa with her family. You can read more of her writing at lisajacksontresch.com and learn about the nonprofit she founded at risingvillage.org.

www.ingramcontent.com/pod-product-compliance
Lightning Source LLC
Chambersburg PA
CBHW020359130626
46549CB00006B/2358